International Standard Book Number ISBN 0-918761-00-X

PRINTED IN THE UNITED STATES OF AMERICA
Published in celebration of Miami University's 175th Anniversary by Miami University, Office of University Publications, Robert H. Hickey, university editor; Tracy L. Chappelow, assistant editor. Illustrated pages and cover designed by Martha J. Hickey.

End papers

front: The way Miami University looked about the time T. C. Hibbett enrolled.

back: The Wharf in Cincinnati, 1848
From the Collection of the Public Library of Cincinnati and Hamilton County

COLLEGE DAYS AT OLD MIAMI:

THE DIARY OF T. C. HIBBETT

1851-1854

EDITED BY

WILLIAM PRATT

PROFESSOR OF ENGLISH

MIAMI UNIVERSITY

MIAMI UNIVERSITY ● OXFORD, OHIO

1984

THIS BOOK IS DEDICATED TO FRANCES NEEL CHENEY,
LIBRARIAN AND TEACHER, WHO GAVE THE HIBBETT
DIARY TO MIAMI UNIVERSITY

Acknowledgements

Besides the indispensable part which Mrs. Brainard ("Fanny")
Cheney played in donating the diary to Miami, she has also contributed letters, photographs, and other documents, some of which are in-
cluded in this book, and a wealth of information about the Hibbett
family and their native towns of Lavergne and Smyrna, Tennessee.
One of T. C. Hibbett's living descendants, Mary Ann Hibbett Andrews
of Nashville, Tennessee, has generously supplied an obituary and a
photograph of her great-grandfather. In addition, the editor has bene-
fited much from the friendship and good counsel of Walter Havighurst, the author of *The Miami Years* and *Men of Old Miami*, whose
books have provided historical background for the characters and
events recorded in T. C. Hibbett's diary, and whose reading of the diary led to much valuable information being uncovered about it. Professor David Frazier, colleague in the English Department and editor of
The Old Northwest journal, read the manuscript of the diary and offered suggestions, and his co-editor, Professor John Dickinson of the
History Department, drew a map of T. C. Hibbett's travels especially
for this publication. Many helpful details have been supplied by other
kind friends, especially by Anne Amos Brown, an alumna of Miami,
and by Robert J. Miller, national secretary of Phi Delta Theta fraternity. The expert help of Frances McClure and Helen Ball in bringing
material to light in the Special Collections Room of the Miami Library, and making it available for publication, is gratefully acknowl-
edged. Finally, a special word of thanks is due to my mother, Irene
Johnston Pratt of Shawnee, Oklahoma, whose support in this project,
as in so many others, has been essential.

T. C. Hibbett's travels back and forth to Miami from his home in Tennessee involved changing from railroad ("cars" as he called them) to stagecoach to steamboat to horse-drawn carriage, or omnibus. This map, drawn by John N. Dickinson, shows graphically the varieties of transportation T. C. Hibbett needed for his week's journey from home to college in the 1850s.

INTRODUCTION

In the summer of 1851, when Theophilus Cannon Hibbett arrived for the first time on the Miami University campus, he found himself facing three spare but substantial brick buildings in the woods near the village of Oxford, with no other student in sight. It could hardly be called a promising start, for a young man who had traveled the better part of five days to enter college — a wearying journey by railroad, stagecoach, steamboat, and horse-drawn omnibus — only to discover when he arrived that he was a month too early for classes. Hibbett was a boy of 17, fresh off the family farm in Tennessee, but he was not easily discouraged; he had come to college well prepared, and after waiting impatiently for the fall term to begin, he proved himself more than ready for his entrance examinations. The professors in those days examined each student individually, in the three subjects of the Classical Humanities curriculum that were the main route to a Bachelor of Arts degree, and they found that in Greek and Mathematics, he was already prepared for the sophomore class, while in Latin, he was enough ahead of the other freshmen to be able, with a little additional study, to qualify as a sophomore in that subject, too. He showed his mettle by deciding to forgo his Christmas holiday at home, and, staying alone in the college dormitory when the rest of the students had gone, brought up his Latin so that he could become a full-fledged sophomore in his second term of college. Such diligence seems to have been characteristic of him, and it paid off well, for he managed to graduate from the university in three years, one of the top scholars in his class, and a leader in both his literary society and his fraternity, the two chief extracurricular activities of college students at Old Miami.

T. C. Hibbett (understandably, he went only by his initials) had the good fortune to come to Miami at the peak of its early promise, when future national leaders such as Benjamin Harrison, David Swing, Whitelaw Reid, and John Shaw Billings were among the small group

of students on the campus, and though he was not destined to bring
fame to his alma mater as they would do, he did become the chroni-
cler who left the most readable account of daily life at Old Miami. Not
that he started the diary with any such purpose in mind: he began it
simply at the suggestion of his father, who had advised him to keep a
record of his youth, "the most important as well as interesting portion
of the short span allotted to man," as he tells himself philosophically
on the first page of the diary, and he kept it up, so it seems, primarily
for his own amusement. Probably no one ever saw the diary during his
lifetime except himself, unless he showed it to his father after his return home in 1854. He was only twenty when he graduated from Miami, and he must have put the diary away with his college memories,
never mentioning it to anyone in later years, because when his obituary was published at the time of his death in 1918, at the age of 84, no
mention was made of his Miami degree (see Appendix C). The diary
might have gone unread forever, but fortunately, a trained librarian
married into the Hibbett family, and her keen eye recognized that the
diary, which had lain neglected in the family attic for a century, was a
valuable first-hand account of an early period of Miami history, and
through her care and generosity, the manuscript of Hibbett's diary
now is safely stored in the Special Collections Room of the Miami library. After over a hundred years in the darkness, it has happily come
to light, in time to be published during the 175th year of Miami's history, giving us a brief but vivid picture of a pioneer American college
in the mid-nineteenth century.

What the Hibbett diary offers is an intimate personal record of one
college student's experience, yet it is typical enough to show us, in the
late twentieth century, just how much higher education has changed,
over the past hundred and thirty years, and it is descriptive enough to
let us relive the experience ourselves, in all its immediacy, its youthful
earnestness, and its often infectious humor. Hard though it is to imagine what Miami was like in its early years, when it was one of the few
institutions of higher learning west of the Appalachians, a small liberal
arts college in frontier Ohio with a half-dozen faculty members and a
few hundred students, through this diary it comes to life again, and
there is much about that life that is still fresh and appealing.

What would have prompted a farm boy in Tennessee to journey all the way to Ohio for a college education? The diary offers no answer to that question, but we can guess that, in the first place, he would not have many colleges to choose from, living in the central United States, west of the mountains, in the period before the Civil War, and among those few, Miami certainly held a leading place. Furthermore, though Miami was not on the main thoroughfares then, or now, it was close enough to the Ohio River to be accessible by steamboat from the rivers of the South, and steamboats were a popular means of travel in the period before the Civil War. The diary does tell us that each time T. C. Hibbett went back and forth to college from his home, he went by steamboat part of the way, and his lively descriptions of the steamboat trip make it obvious that he relished this adventurous form of transportation — much as today's college students might enjoy traveling by airplane. But most importantly, Hibbett had a teacher in Tennessee who influenced him to choose Miami, and who, the diary tells us, accompanied him on his first trip to the campus. The teacher and friend was Robert Morrison, a Miami graduate of 1849, and one of the founders of the Phi Delta Theta fraternity, who after his graduation had gone to Poplar Grove Academy in Rutherford County, Tennessee, near Hibbett's home, to become first teacher and then principal. Morrison was no longer a Miami student, but he had the instinctive urge of the loyal alumnus to return to his Alma Mater, was always on the lookout for prospective students to enroll in the college, and was even willing, in Hibbett's case, to escort him all the way to the campus. Though Hibbett never explains why he chose Miami, Robert Morrison is mentioned often in the diary, and we can assume that it was his personal influence which counted most in bringing one of his star pupils from Tennessee to Ohio, just as we can suppose that Morrison was mainly responsible for preparing Hibbett so well that he entered as a virtual sophomore rather than a mere freshman.

Morrison may have directed him to Miami, but he was not the only student from his region on the campus when he arrived. There were many other students from the South in Hibbett's time at Miami, as we know from his mention of friends from Tennessee, Georgia, Mississippi and Kentucky, and indeed, the diary gives a strong impression that sectional rivalry, only a decade before the Civil War split the country apart, caused surprisingly little concern to the young men at Miami.

What most concerned them was the bond of brotherhood, which knit the two hundred or so students together into literary societies first and college fraternities second — and not into regional associations at all. Hibbett joined the Union Literary Society his first year, and Phi Delta Theta fraternity his second year, and the rivalry that developed between the Union, Erodelphian, and Eccritean Societies, and between the Beta Theta Pis, Phi Delta Thetas, and Alpha Delta Phis, was much more fierce than any sectional rivalries the students of Old Miami might have felt. The diary is especially valuable in the continuing narrative it gives of the interplay between debating societies and fraternities, at the time when Miami was fostering both kinds of activity among its students. In time, the debating societies would fade away and the fraternities would flourish, but when Hibbett was at Miami, both were going strong, and he played a central role in each, and clearly enjoyed the opportunities for friendly argument and sociable conversation which each afforded.

In the Union Literary Society, Hibbett participated actively throughout his three years, serving as Recording Secretary in his second year and as Corresponding Secretary in his last year, and he noted in his diary the weekly topics of debate that he and his classmates vigorously argued with each other. Educational issues that provoked spirited discussion in the 1850s were: "Should the education of the sexes be separate?"; "Should the dead languages receive the attention they now do in our colleges?" Political questions could also raise controversy: "Is the Union endangered by Roman Catholicism?", "Should the United States intervene on behalf of Hungary?" And racial discrimination was as troublesome a topic then as now: "Has the Indian been treated worse than the white man?", "Should free Negroes be permitted to settle in the state?" It was customary at "hall" meetings for speakers on both sides of an issue to be heard, and then a vote taken of the members to decide whether the Affirmative or Negative had won. Hibbett took part in these weekly debates with enthusiasm, but he reserved his greatest interest for the annual Exhibition, held each December at the end of the fall term, which was a public speaking event that drew a large audience from Oxford and the surrounding towns. In one of his most extended narratives in the diary, he gives a humorous blow-by-blow account of the Union Literary Exhibition of 1853, when

he and five other speakers nervously took the stand in the Old School
Presbyterian Church, accompanied by the Acton Brass Band, and
alternately bored or diverted the audience, estimated at about a thou-
sand people, for more than three hours. It was in many respects the
high point of his college career, although he had the further honor of
giving one of the Commencement addresses for his graduating class in
June of 1854.

As for the college fraternities, Hibbett entered Miami in the period
when they were outlawed, as an aftermath of the Snowball Rebellion
of 1848, and though he had been brought to the campus by one of the
founders of Phi Delta Theta, he refused an invitation to join the fraternity in his first year, choosing instead to participate in a mock-
fraternity organized to ridicule the secret fraternities at Miami. But
President Anderson relented, and allowed the fraternities official recognition at the Commencement of 1852, and in his second year, Hibbett accepted the invitation to join Phi Delta Theta, which was then so
large that it met in two separate chapters in the college dormitories.
He was elected secretary of the fraternity in the spring of 1853, and
president the next fall, and he makes note of the fact that Phi Delta
Theta sent one of its initiates to start a chapter at Austin College in
Texas, and so was fast becoming a national fraternity while he was in
college. The purpose of the fraternity was primarily social, and fast
friendships were formed, but it could also be a political force on campus, as we learn from Hibbett's notes that the "Phis" were accused of
controlling elections in the Union Literary Society and were attacked
by their main rivals, the "Betas." Between the lines of the diary, we
can detect that the literary societies were beginning to yield popularity
to the social fraternities, as they did later on in Miami history, although
in Hibbett's college years both were equally indispensable to the kind
of education he sought, which was intellectual, moral, and social, a
blend of learning, discussion, and friendship.

A further side of college life which emerges most appealingly from
the diary was the very close friendship between the faculty and the
students. After all, there were only seven faculty members at Miami in
Hibbett's day, including the president, and with only about two hundred students to teach, there was ample occasion for students and professors to become well acquainted. Moreover, Dr. William C. Ander-

son, who had taken over as Miami's fourth president in 1849, after the
ranks of students had been decimated by the Snowball Rebellion of
1848, made sure that the faculty would be in closer touch with students than before, by installing Charles Elliott, the Greek professor,
along with Mrs. Elliott, in the North Dormitory, where they often invited students, among them T. C. Hibbett, to tea in their rooms. President Anderson himself presided over the required chapel service every morning that started the school day, and Professor Robert H.
Bishop, Jr., son of the first Miami president, was in charge of keeping
the students' money safe while they were in Oxford. Thus the students
and their professors shared not only the classroom but the college life,
and the diary shows that there was both respect and affection between
them. Hibbett notes more than once that "Old Bobby" Bishop was his
favorite professor, with whom he often exchanged reading matter, and
he argued religious points with Dr. Anderson, sometimes heatedly;
one of the most touching moments of his college career came at his
parting with Dr. Anderson after commencement, when, he says, the
president was "perfectly childish" in his reluctance to say goodbye to
the students and leave Miami, only five years after he had come to restore confidence and build enrollment in the university. Whatever
gains Miami has made in the size of its faculty and student body in the
intervening century, some of the friendly intercourse between them
has inevitably been lost, at any rate as a daily experience of living together outside the classroom as well as inside it, in the easy way
Hibbett's account brings to mind.

Hibbett's roommates during his three years at Miami did not have
as far to travel to college as he did, since each of them came from
towns near Oxford. The first was William H. R. Honnell of Sidney,
Ohio, who stayed only a short while before returning home to teach,
but came back to Miami later to finish his degree, and then went on to
seminary, where he became in time the Rev. Wm. Honnell. He served
as chaplain to a cavalry regiment in the Civil War, and afterwards
wrote an eyewitness account of the efforts to check Morgan's Raid, the
most celebrated skirmish by Confederate troops across the Mason-
Dixon line; Honnell was with the Union forces which chased Morgan
and his men through Indiana, Ohio, and Kentucky before finally cap-
turing them. After the Civil War, Honnell moved to Kansas, where he

died in 1895. Hibbett's second roommate was E. W. McCartey of Brookville, Indiana, who also left college before the year was out, going to seek opportunities in St. Paul, Minnesota, from which outpost he wrote an amusing letter back to his old roommate at Miami about the wild Minnesota frontier (see Appendix A.2). Hibbett's last "roomy" in the North Dormitory was James R. Patterson of Hamilton, Ohio, who became a brother Phi Delta Theta in college, and who went on to become a highly successful businessman after college, maintaining residences in Louisiana and Ohio, and building a fine house in Oxford which he called Glenwilde, but which is today called Patterson Place, presently the headquarters of the Western College Alumnae Association, while the street in front of it also bears the name of Patterson Avenue. Patterson served as a trustee of the university for many years, was a generous patron of the library, and was awarded an honorary degree by his alma mater in 1912, the year before his death.

Though Miami was a small college, and Oxford a village, compared to today's university and town, the condition in which Hibbett found them in the fall of 1851 was in many respects a highly favorable one, as we can judge by a column which appeared in the nearby newspaper, the *Hamilton Intelligencer*, on October 30, 1851:

Oxford — Its Improvements — Institutions of Learning, &c.
During a short visit to the pleasant town of Oxford, in this county, we were much pleased to note the unmistakeable evidences of its increased prosperity. Situated on an eminence, beautifully sloping in every direction, Oxford occupies one of the most desirable and pleasant locations in the country, and it would be strange if its beauties were passed by unnoticed by the pleasure-seeker from the smoky, dingy city. In every direction from Oxford a splendid country spreads out in magnificent prospect, reminding one of the descriptions of oriental splendor and grandeur.
We noticed that during the past year, the spirit of improvement has seized upon some of the business men of the place, and that several large, fine buildings have been erected. Among others may be noticed one just completed by Messrs. Hills and Kumler, containing four splendid business rooms below, all of which are occupied by enterprising men — the corner one by the owners of the building as a Dry Goods store, which will favorably compare with any establishment of the kind we have lately seen,

the entire stock having been selected in the east with great care and taste, and sold at very moderate prices. We are happy to learn that the business of these merchants is steadily on the increase. The upper story is occupied as a Masonic Hall, and is, we understand, fitted up with good taste. On the whole, we are inclined to the opinion, that business of every kind has very much improved in Oxford during the year past, and the "signs of the times" plainly indicate that the summit of her glory has not yet been attained.

Miami University, which, some two years since, had a decided downward tendency, is now, under the supervision and control of its present excellent President, Dr. Anderson, rapidly assuming her former position among the literary lights of the present age. The number of students now enrolled is 170, being an increase over the last session of between 80 and 90, the largest number we are informed, ever enrolled during a single session, even in her palmiest days. The Miami Valley needs a good institution of this kind, and we hope that the new life and vigor infused into old "Miami University" may never again die away as in former years.

The Female Institute, under the control of Dr. Scott, promises fair to supply a deficiency that has long existed in Female education. The number of young ladies in actual attendance is 125, and constantly increasing. We were very much pleased with the course pursued in this institution, and hope it may long remain an honor to the town where it is situated, a lasting benefit to the young ladies of the West, to our country, and to the world. Female education is beginning to assume its proper place, and we rejoice that it is so. It is but another evidence of the progress of Christianity, and its influence will be felt for better upon generations yet unborn.

There are many other interesting things about Oxford which we would like to notice, but must reserve them for another time.

It is apparent from this account that the town and college were both enjoying new growth and prosperity at the time Hibbett entered Miami, and it is also apparent that the college boys were not entirely isolated from the fairer sex, since the Female Institute which Dr. Scott had brought to Oxford in 1849 had almost as many students as Miami University. Hibbett's diary mentions that there were ladies present in some of the chapel services — sometimes causing a disturbance, as an early entry notes that Dr. Anderson's sermon was interrupted by a barking dog, which had jumped down from the lap of its young mistress and broken up the service — and he refers to their presence at other public occasions, such as the annual speech-making Exhibitions of the literary societies, and at Commencement exercises. We can judge from the fact that Dr. Scott's daughter Caroline married Benjamin Harrison, soon after his graduation from Miami in 1852, that relations between the boys' and girls' colleges were often more than just friendly.

Another aspect of Old Miami which the newspaper article calls attention to is the strong influence of religion on college life. Not even the resurgence of Christian groups on campus in recent years can begin to compare with the strongly evangelical spirit evident in the early years of Miami, as reflected throughout the diary. All the presidents of Miami, from the beginning until after the Civil War, were Presbyterian ministers, and there was such revivalism on campus in Hibbett's day that he mentions going to chapel every day and church twice on Sunday, with frequent prayer meetings interspersed. Many of his classmates were preparing for the ministry, and he heard one sermon at the Old School Presbyterian Church on "the obligation of Christians to become ministers in preference to other professions." Of his particular friends at Miami, David Swing was already an ordained minister, and Robert Morrison would soon become a minister, and he corresponded at times with other classmates who had gone from Miami to Princeton Divinity School. Though Hibbett himself apparently did not seriously think of a religious career, his diary indicates that he read the Bible almost daily, and that his life at college was as much concerned with religious and moral education as with academic learning.

If T. C. Hibbett had a professional career in mind, he does not mention it in his diary, and all we know of his ambitions after college we get from a letter he received from a cousin in Tennessee (see Appendix A.1), which mentions the possibility of a teaching position, but rather discourages the idea. Hibbett was a serious student bent on getting a liberal education while he was at Miami, and he succeeded well in that aim, graduating near the top of his class. He must have been one of the best speakers as well as scholars in his class, judging by his choice for the Exhibition of the Union Literary Society in his senior year, and his honor as one of the Commencement speakers in 1854. President Anderson wanted him to have the distinction of speaking in French at Commencement, but thought better of the idea, since he suspected that few in the Commencement audience would understand him. Certainly he was gifted at learning languages, adding to the Greek and Latin that were required for his degree the elective subjects of German and French. And his reading was prodigious, as the diary clearly shows: he went through the collected works of Washington Irving, his favorite living author, and read volumes of English history and biography, as well as the poetry of Byron and the satires of Swift, while keeping current with the issues of the popular *Knickerbocker* magazine which were sent to him by his father. He also read best-sellers such as Charles Dickens' *David Copperfield,* Harriet Beecher Stowe's *Uncle Tom's Cabin,* and the works of "Ik Marvel," an admired author of the day. The fact that Professor Elliott chose him in his senior year to serve as sub-librarian shows that his professors looked on him as one of the best-read members of his class, and his friends showed their respect by giving him as graduation presents the works of Shakespeare, Byron, and Macaulay. The evidence of a lively and inquiring mind is on every page of Hibbett's diary, and shows that the old-fashioned Classical Humanities education was by no means limited to ancient studies.

There is another value of the old liberal arts curriculum which the diary consistently reveals: the ability to write intelligently and gracefully. Hibbett's prose style is formal by today's standards, but quite varied in mood and form, ranging from light verse to humorous narrative, and from self-criticism to "purple patches" of elegance (note especially his lavish description of a sunrise, seen from the window of his room in Elliott Hall, entered in the diary on Nov. 23rd, 1851). His vocabulary was large, from the day he began his diary at the age of seventeen, and he had the good sense to compress his entries more and more as the diary progressed, to avoid boring himself with repetition of trivia and to record only the more significant events of his college years. The finest sustained passage in the diary is his account of the trip home by steamboat after his first year at Miami, which includes descriptions of characters he met and scenes he observed along the Ohio and Cumberland rivers, almost fit to stand comparison with the *Sketch-Book* of his favorite author, Washington Irving. Indeed, Hib-

bett's writing does exhibit a lively style, with personal flavor and interest all along, and it is evident that his reading of contemporary writers
like Irving influenced his own diction and gave charm and sophistica-
tion to his account of the brief three years of his college career. There
emerges from the diary a recognizable and appealing personality, with
sound common sense and an effervescent sense of humor, and it
seems remarkable that he should not have found a vocation as a writer
some time later in life.

Certainly Hibbett had enough independence of mind and conscience, for the diary shows that he was quite aware of holding views
different from his classmates on many issues. In the entry of Jan. 3rd
& 4th, 1853, he notes that he is writing a speech for the Union Literary Society about Thomas Paine, that radical pamphleteer of the Rev-
olutionary era in American politics, and says that "My views of this
individual, I know, are not orthodox; nevertheless, I live in a free country, and the object of my life is not to please the world by going against
my conscience to advocate what the majority believe." This is by no
means the sole example of Hibbett's individualism, for when his fellow
students catch what he calls "the Kossuth fever," and petition the faculty to dismiss classes at Miami so that they can attend the Hungarian
patriot's public address in Hamilton, Hibbett calmly remains alone in
the dormitory, feeling that he would rather study his Greek and Latin
than spend his time listening to a contemporary political figure, however exciting the occasion might be. His independence extended to religious matters, as well as political, for when the college is experienc-
ing a revivalist fervor and classes are deserted for prayer meetings
around the clock, he continues to work at his studies and meet his
classes, noting that he cannot justify neglecting his study even if the
cause seems as serious as saving one's soul. Throughout his diary,
Hibbett appears as a young man with remarkable self-assurance and
strength of conviction, quite content to go his own way rather than follow the crowd.

There is a sense, in fact, in which the diary seems almost planned: it
has a commendable unity as well as brevity about it, as though the author intended that it should begin as he left home for college, and end
as he made his way homeward after his college days were over. Both
the opening and closing scenes, when he parts from his family at

home, and when he parts from his friends and professors at college, are somewhat sad occasions, and his reluctance to go in each case shows his naturally sentimental attachment to familiar faces and surroundings. The companion who left home with him, Robert Morrison, is also waiting to greet him at the steamboat dock in Louisville on his homeward journey, and so seems like a guardian, or guide, during this important maturing period, or rite of passage, in his life. It is true that there are monotonous and trivial incidents in the diary, which he would undoubtedly have eliminated if he had edited the diary for publication himself — particularly the frequent anxieties about his health, which on the whole seems remarkably robust, considering that his only severe ailments in three years were two tooth extractions and a case of measles — but he recognized before the end of his first year that he needed to be more succinct, and there is a corresponding gain in economy at that point. If he had really planned the diary, it would not have the spontaneity and authenticity it displays, but compared to other diaries of Miami students of his day, its brevity and unity give it distinction, and an almost professional air of self-direction makes it seem complete, in spite of its being a highly selective record of only three years out of a long life. We know at least from the amusing column which he wrote, in the middle of his senior year, for the *Hamilton Intelligencer*, entitled "The Sub-Freshman's Composition," that he did think of himself as a writer at times, and the diary is proof enough that he might have made a name for himself if he had chosen to become a professional writer later on.

That he did not use his writing skill after his college years at Miami seems a pity, but he had other responsibilities to attend to. We know little about his later life, except that he went to Cumberland Law School in Tennessee, was admitted to the bar in 1857, and practiced law for four years until the Civil War broke out in 1861. He then volunteered and served in the infantry of the Confederacy, until he was captured in the battle of Fort Donelson, not far from his home in Tennessee, in 1862. He was exchanged after a few months as a prisoner of war, and rose to the rank of Captain and Provost-Marshal in Bate's Division of the Army of Tennessee. When he returned to civilian life, he served as a civil engineer, and also as Justice of the Peace, though his obituary makes no mention of these positions, simply listing his local

reputations as a farmer, a Mason, and "devout member of the Presbyterian church." Although his obituary is silent about the Miami connection, his loyalty to his Alma Mater is evident on every page of the
diary, particularly at the end, where he mused to himself, as he waited
for the stagecoach to take him home, from the door of Mrs. Hughes's
boarding house across from the campus, "I regretted leaving Oxford
very much, as I never expect to see it again." He did not see it again,
but he wrote to his "kindly remembered preceptor," "Old Bobby"
Bishop, in 1887, when the doors of Miami had opened once more, and
Old Miami had become New Miami: "I am so glad to know that the
University still lives and I sincerely hope she may more than regain
her former status among the first colleges of the land." Such a feeling,
and such a wish, surely connects the Miami graduate of 1854 with the
Miami graduate of 1984, whatever differences there may be in the size
and character of the institution that inspires their loyalty to its past and
their hopes for its future. Tradition means change, but it also means
continuity: Miami, fortunately, has known plenty of both in its first 175
years, and that is why it goes on enduring, in the minds of today's grad-
uates as it clearly did in the mind of a graduate of 130 years ago,
"among the first colleges of the land."

1852   *91*

June 5th I was up at 4 oclock so as to be ready for the stage and carried my trunk over to Mrs Hughs; as that was the place the agents agreed to instruct the driver of the Omnibus to call for me but he forgot to tell him, and I was left: so I went to the Livery stable and hired a horse and buggy & Mr Brown went with me to Hamilton to bring the same back, arrived at Hamilton about 9 AM and took the cars from that place to Cincinnati; when I got to the depot the Omnibus driver, in a great hurry, took my trunk and left me, & I thought I had seen my trunk for the last time: I hired an omnibus and went to the "Broad way Hotel" and after about an hours search found my trunk. My next business was to find a boat going to Nashville. but there was not one on the wharf that would start before the next evening: as the weather was quite cool, and it had been raining all day and was very wet, I began to get sick of my trip and wished I had waited till some of the college boys were coming down this way: Made arrangements with the clerk on the boat Jenny Lind to take me to Nashville for 10 and went on board

T. C. Hibbett's penmanship was exemplary throughout the diary, as this manuscript page shows. It is the beginning of his account of returning home from Oxford in June of 1852, after his first year of college, when the stagecoach failed to pick him up at the door of Mrs. Hughes' boarding house, and he had to hire a horse and buggy for the trip to Hamilton, where he caught the train to Cincinnati, and then, for $10, bought passage on the steamboat Jenny Lind *all the way from Cincinnati to Nashville.*

COLLEGE DAYS AT OLD MIAMI:
THE DIARY OF T. C. HIBBETT
1851-54

*Robert Morrison had been T. C. Hibbett's teacher
at Poplar Grove Academy in Tennessee, and accompanied him on his first trip to the Miami campus in 1851. Morrison had helped found Phi Delta
Theta fraternity in his room in the North Dorm
(now Elliott Hall) in 1848, and after a few years as
a teacher in Tennessee, he was ordained as a Presbyterian minister and served in Kentucky and
Missouri.*

Oxford Nov. 18th 1851
Having received a letter from my father, J. F. Hibbett, dated Oct.
30th, in which he expressed a desire that I should, at the end of each
day make a record of what I had done that day, and by so doing, I
would not only preserve my youthful deeds and thoughts, but, as youth
is the most important as well as interesting portion of the short span
allotted to man, it would also be a great consolation in after life to look
back on that time when the mind is generally occupied in building airy
castles and stored with vain imaginations concerning the future. Under such considerations I begin the present work. It would, however,
have been more proper to have begun such a work at the commencement of my collegiate course; but as it has thus far been omitted
through negligence, I will advert to and only give a short sketch of
what has transpired from the time I left home until the present.

July 14th
After several days spent in meditations as to my future course and
prospects, the atrabilarian[1] moment at last, to my sorrow, arrived: in
which I was to bid adieu to all that I could call relations and friends,
and when for the first time in my life I was to say, farewell sweet home.
Having bid adieu to my father's family, in company with my brothers,
James and Ira, I went to the railroad, there meeting Robt. Morrison,[2]
who was destined to the same place with myself; we took the cars to
Nashville, where we arrived about sunset; having a good deal of business to attend to we did not retire to rest until about mid-night.
Weather exceedingly warm.

July 15.
Left Nashville at 4 a.m. by stage for Louisville, coach crowded, weath-
er warm, and roads very dusty; took breakfast just before arriving at
Gallatin, after passing which place, the country gradually became
more and more broken until it seemed, in comparison with Ruther-
ford County, a mountainous wilderness. We took dinner at Scottsville,
Allen County, Kentucky, which is a village of very little importance;
from thence we traveled through Barren County and took supper at
Glasgow. The land of Barren County is greatly superior to that of
Allen, about equal to that of Sumner County, Tennessee.

July 16.

After traveling all the previous night, we stopped at a farmer's cottage, whence after having taken some refreshment, we resumed our journey. The appearance of the country around Bardstown, and indeed from that to Louisville, is truly picturesque. Oh, what a charming sight to one just emerging from the inarable wilds of interior Kentucky! We arrived at Louisville, which is a very beautiful city, at 6 p.m.

July 17.

Rising very early, I divert myself in traveling over Louisville until 11 a.m., at which time I set out by steamboat for Cincinnati.

July 18.

Waked very early, and, very much to my surprise, was landed on the Cincinnati wharf. After securing my trunk I went up in the city, but being very unwell from riding in the boat, I did not enjoy the pleasure of viewing the city very extensively, but as soon as possible secured my passage, by way of Omnibus,[3] to Oxford, where for the first time in my life I could freely like one of old say that I was a stranger in a strange land. This was to me the beginning of trouble, for when I found that the next college term did not begin until the last Monday in August, it increased my melancholy feelings very much to think that all this time was to be spent without having anything to do, and with which to divert my mind, for the Professors were all absent and therefore I could have no particular study from not knowing in what class I would be put.

July 21.

Rent a room in one of the college buildings and furnish it for a study room, though I took no very particular delight in staying in it during vacation, as it was situated in a very large building in which there was no one except myself, which rendered it quite lonesome. Boarding at Tavern.

August 1st.

Getting somewhat over my home-sickness, though time as yet seemed to pass very slowly and my thoughts will, in spite of every effort to pre-

vent it, be occupied in scenes concerning home: somewhat in this
manner.

Home

I love to muse on thee.
And think of pleasures past.
Can that time ever be?
And will it come at last?

When I'll be forced to say
I have no home at all
Oh! Take the thought away
It's pungent more than gall.

Home though 'tis a poor one,
Is a solace for grief,
And who beneath the sun
Is not of this belief?

Home, I knew not thy worth,
Till to part we were forced.
I thought not of thy mirth,
Till my journey was coursed.

For what have I left you!
Education I say.
To make my brain anew
There is no other way.

When this I shall procure,
Then surely I'll come back.
I'm no longer demure
When homewards I can track.

Even in Arabia's waste,
Or Afric's parching sand;
I'd quicker to thee haste
Than if some coral strand.

Yet fain would I now come,
But know it will not do!
Fain would I courage sum
And hasten there to you.

Had I the wheels of time,
I'd make swifter its gait.
Ere I could pen this rhyme,
It would grow very late.

But 'tis a foolish thought,
To wish for power, such
'Twould bring the world to nought
For me to do so much.

To be content I'll try,
My time I will not waste;
The time is truly nigh
When I again can taste

The pleasure just in being
At home, and friends seeing.

August 21.

The Professors having returned, I pay them a visit in order to hear in what class they would put me. First, Professor J. C. Moffatt[4] of Latin: I was prepared for the Sophomore class as far as the amount of reading was concerned, except Livy, and on this account was compelled to enter the Freshman class. Next, to the Professor of Greek, Charles Elliott[5]: on examination, I was permitted to enter the Freshman class, but after reciting three or four lessons, was advanced to the Sophomore class, with a promise to read up what was required of the Freshman class. Then to Prof. T. J. Matthews[6] of Mathematics: on examination, I was permitted to enter the Sophomore class with a promise to bring up Surveying.

Aug. 25.
The students having collected, i.e., the greater portion of them, we
met in Chapel, and after a prayer by the President W. C. Anderson,[7]
the Professors retired to their respective rooms and examined the new
students, after which they adjourned until next morning at 8 o'clock.
From that time until the present I have been applying myself closely
to my books, though I have not accomplished as much as I had expected in the beginning. My health has been tolerably good most of
the time, though I have had an attack occasioned by too close application and not a sufficiency of exercise.

Nov. 23rd. Sabbath.
The king of day triumphantly arose from behind the Eastern horizon,
as if he had been in eager anxiety awaiting the moment in which his
Director would command him to his diurnal duty: all nature seems to
leap for joy at his welcome advent, as if conscious that it was his design
to free her from the cold that had spread its congealing influence and
enclosed her in its glaciating grasp: the scene was truly beautiful. But
alas! Ere he had traversed one third of his course, his glittering coun-
tenance was again shut out from us by thick clouds threatening snow.
Thus the day passed by, wearing somewhat of a gloomy aspect. I heard
a sermon delivered in chapel by W. C. Anderson, D. D., the President
of the College; his sermon was as usual very interesting and instructive. My health is not very good from sitting up all night to learn the
preface of Livy; my other lessons were also more difficult and longer,
and from my present feelings I think that hereafter I shall go to bed at
eleven o'clock, whether I know my lessons or not.

Nov. 24.
A very beautiful day: bearing very much the resemblance of Spring,
and from the cheerful aspect of the weather and having had a refreshing night's sleep, I feel very much better than for some time past.

Nov. 25.
From the appearance of the weather on last evening, one would very
naturally have been led to the conclusion that we would be favored, at
least for a while, with pleasant times as respects cold; but it has proved

far different: for after getting out of bed this morning, greatly to my surprise I beheld the ground covered with snow, and it has snowed all day without ceasing, until about dark, when it became very clear and cold. I have made very passable recitations today, although Livy lessons were very long. I have a very severe pain in my breast, and in consequence of which have not studied very much, but hope by going to bed early I can rise early in the morning and make up lost time. My roommate, Wm. H. R. Honnell of Sidney, Ohio, left me this evening; he is going home to teach until the beginning of next term. I have bought his share of the room and intend to get another roommate as soon as I can find one that I think will suit me.

Nov. 26.
The sun shone out beautifully all day, though not with sufficient force to make the weather by any means pleasant. My recitations for this day were barely passable. The pain in my breast is somewhat abated. Received a letter from brother Ira which afforded great comfort.

Nov. 27.
This is the day appointed by the Governor of the state of Ohio for thanksgiving for the many fold blessings that it has been the will of our Creator to bestow upon us, and as our College is a state institution, with the permission of the President and Professors we have no school, but instead the President delivered a sermon in Chapel; a very interesting occasion; although there was preaching in all the other churches in town, the Chapel was crowded. Some of the students seemed to think that the President meddled where it was very unbecoming in him, because his text naturally led him into politics; he however said nothing disrespectful, and in fact said but little about it in any way; what he said however was in favor of the Whigs.[8] I have spent the day in preparing my lessons for tomorrow and writing a composition for the Society. There is a donation party this evening at the Rev. Mr. Tenny's, the pastor of the New School Presbyterian Church[9]; the donation is to Mrs. Tenny. I do not attend, thinking it the more prudent plan, for one who does not enjoy very good health, to stay by the fire, especially during such unfavorable weather; though I should be very much pleased to attend, having never witnessed such a performance.

Nov. 28.

Nothing of any importance has transpired during this day. I made passable recitations, and feel moderately well, except for a bad cold taken on the previous evening from having sat up after my fire had almost entirely gone out. The hall met this evening, which meeting was the time for the passing of an amendment to the Constitution and By-laws. I, thinking that such an amendment was not for the best interest of the hall, opposed it and debated for a time, but as the hall was almost unanimously opposed to me, when the vote was taken it passed by a large majority; after attending to what irregular business was before the hall we adjourned until after supper. After we had met after supper, the following question was with some interest discussed and decided in favor of the Negative side, "Is neutrality the true policy of the United States?", after which I attend the Censors meeting and handed in my composition for criticism.

Nov. 29.

Spend this day in sawing wood and other kinds of exercise: feel very unwell in the evening and retire to bed very early. E. M. McCartey from Franklin County, Indiana, came in this morning as a roommate.

Nov. 30th.

The weather being very disagreeable, I stay by the fire all day except to go to the preaching in Chapel, Dr. Anderson officiating. The Dr. had taken a text which afforded an extensive field for sound reasoning, also one from which there was much instruction to be derived, and when he had gotten a little more than half through his discourse there was a lap dog that ran out and commenced barking at the Dr. at such a furious rate that he requested the owner to take it out; the owner not making his or rather her appearance, Professor Elliott undertook to drive the dog out but failed in the attempt; so the Dr. dismissed the congregation with the request that they would bring no more dogs to church, a very fair request.

Dec. 1st.

Weather clear but cold. My bad cold getting somewhat better, and spirits a little revived from having received a letter from my friend and classmate at Poplar Grove Academy, P. C. G. Kimbro, which contained very cheering news. There was a call meeting of the Miami Union Literary Society[10] in order to attend to some business concerning an exhibition of said Society to take place on the 18th.

Dec. 2nd.

Snowed and sleeted nearly all day, though it was very little colder than it was on the preceding day: yet from the tune that the wind is now singing around my room it will be very cold before morning. My recitations were all very good today except Latin; this however was passable. I have almost entirely gotten over my cold.

Dec. 3.

Weather cold and disagreeable, which seems to cast a gloomy feeling over me. I have been out in the cold almost half the day, which has by no means been conducive to my good health; at least I know no other cause to which I can attribute the pain that is in my breast. Recitations have all been very good today. From my indisposition, time, (and, I am glad to say that this is the first time that I have had such a feeling lately) hangs exceedingly heavy; not that I am homesick, but am anxious for vacation to come when I can rest from my studies.

Dec. 4th.

The first part of this day was spent to very little purpose; I feeling very unwell as to my body, which caused my mind to be in such a state as to unfit me for study, my recitations were barely passable; however, the latter part of the day was better spent, partly in bringing up what was behind.

Dec. 5.

Have no mathematical lesson today, for some reason the Professor not coming to recitation. The class as usual at the ringing of the 9 o'clock bell went to recitation, but the Professor had not dismissed the Senior class which recited at that hour. So our class after waiting about five minutes ran off from recitation, it being too cold to wait longer. My Latin recitation at 11 was better than usual. The Society met this evening; the regular business having been dispensed with, the Society then proceeded to the investigation of Mr. John M. Worden's case, who had been arraigned before the Society in the first place for absence of three successive meetings: and in the second place for having used disrespectful language in reference to the Society. The prosecuting attorney was Jos. McNutt, and Milton Saylor his assistant; the defendant was Henry Helm, with Pollard Morgan for his assistant. After sufficient trial the Society decided the said John M. Worden to be guilty of the charges alleged, and also decided that the penalty inflicted should be presidential reprimand, which however is to be given at a future meeting. At the evening session there are very few of the members present, there being preaching in all the churches in town; the regular business having been dispensed with, the Society entered into election of some from their number to address the Society at the second meeting of the next session, the result of which was, viz., J. McNutt, S. Hibbern, J. Brooks, H. Denny, and MGS Atherton.

Dec. 6.
Weather clear and moderately cold. Health better today than usual. My lessons for Monday being very easy, I spend the day in sawing wood and other kinds of exercise, from which I feel exceedingly wearied and expect to retire to bed early. I have gotten me a gas lamp, with which I am very much pleased, as it gives a far better light than my former oil one and besides it is not so filthy and I think no more expensive.

Dec. 7.
Weather still warm, though cloudy tonight, and it is probable that there will be rain before morning. Health still good and spirits very much revived. Stay in my room all day except to attend meals and go to preaching in the Chapel, the Rev. Mr. Tenny, the pastor of the New School Presbyterian church, officiating, who preached a practicable sermon and one which was very well suited to the occasion.

Dec. 8.
Weather comfortable cold and health much better than usual; recitations quite creditable. Ran off from Professor Moffatt's recitation, although he was in the recitation room within a few minutes after the bell quit ringing.

Dec. 9.

Weather quite warm for the season, until about sunset, when it commenced sleeting and grew very cold. Recitations very good. Have the headache, otherwise entirely well.

Dec. 10th.

Weather cold and cloudy, indicative of snow. Recitations very passable, though nothing to boast of. The Sophomore Class send up a petition to the faculty to have their examination on the 11th instead of the 17th, the decision concerning which has not been given, but will be at the next diurnal meeting of the faculty which is at 7:30 o'clock a.m. Health only moderately good. Receive a letter from Robt. Morrison, the principal of Poplar Grove Academy, Rutherford County, Tennessee. Finish review in Greek under Professor Charles Elliott.

Dec. 11th.

Weather about the same as the preceding day. Recitations barely passable. Received a visit in room from Professor Elliott, who invited me to take tea with him at 5:30 o'clock on the evening of the 12th.

Dec. 12th.

The examinations of the students began today, commencing with Professor Bishop,[11] in the preparatory department. Society met this evening; after dispensing with the regular business the Society proceeded to the election of an anniversary speaker. (Mr. W. B. Preston of South Carolina was elected some time since, who was so informed by our Corresponding Secretary, through a letter, but as we, after having sufficient time, have received no answer, we have given over getting him, and his alternate, Henry S. Foote of Mississippi, having been elected Governor of that state, cannot come.) The result of the election was, viz., for principal, the Rev. Mr. McGill of Pittsburgh; for alternate, Rev. Mr. Green of Princeton. Take tea with Professor Charles Elliott. I am very well entertained, as the Professor and his wife are very sociable and attractive company.

Dec. 13th.

Weather very cold and disagreeable. Pass my examination in Latin, which was very good. I am also examined in Greek; in this I did tolerably well, which however was better than I expected. My health is not very good; no particular complaint, but feel debilitated as to my body from long confinement.

Dec. 14th.
Weather extremely cold: stayed in my room all day, did not attend preaching even in the Chapel. Mind very restless. Read a portion of the Bible in Job.

Dec. 15.
Weather still cold, ground covered with snow. I had to pull my wood from under the snow and saw it before I could have a fire; I became very cold. Received a letter from my friend J. F. Bailey, in which he stated that my Father granted me the privilege to come home if I so wished, but as I have some back studies to bring up in vacation, I think it would be better to stay and study.

Dec. 16th.
Weather clear and very cold; although the sun shone out all day, there was no sign of the snow melting, which now covers the ground. Spend the day in reviewing Analytical Geometry and answering some letters, saw some wood this evening. The Miami Union Literary Society have an exhibition this evening.

Dec. 17th.
Weather same, if any difference colder. Am examined in Analytical Geometry, get through very well, attend an exhibition of the Erodelphian Society. The exhibition of the Miami Union having been on the evening of the 16th, both were well conducted. There being four speeches from each Society, the house was crowded.

Dec. 18.
Weather same. Health not as good as it has been for the last three or four days. Answer the letter from my friend J. F. Bailey. As yesterday was the last day of our examination, the greater part of the boys go home and the College seems almost deserted.

Dec. 19.

Weather about same, spend the day in reading part of Horace's *Epistle to the Pisos*. Take a very bad cold, also have the headache. The few students remaining here met in the Miami Union Hall and resolved to have a regular weekly debate. We chose the following question, "Should the U.S. support military schools?", which was debated with some interest.

Dec. 20.

Weather a little moderated, though it becomes cloudy in the evening and commences snowing. Am very lonesome, as my roommate went home today. Read a little Latin in Horace and take a walk in the evening. My cold no better, and is also accompanied with a cough.

> Oh time! Thou slow-paced,
> Linger not, but haste.
> Of speed be not shy:
> Slow hours, soon pass by.

Dec. 21st.

Weather cold and cloudy; everything seems dreary and dull; stay by the fire all day; my cold not better and cough seems worse, and under these circumstances pass the day with great uneasiness of mind and ill feelings as to my body; think much of my future prospects, and my past transactions.

Dec. 22.

Weather cold but fair. Read part of Homer's *Iliad* in the forenoon, and in the afternoon write a letter to Miss Jane E. Miller, after which read part of Horace's *Epistle to the Pisos*. Health about the same.

Dec. 23.

Weather same. Read part of Homer and Horace. Receive a letter from brother Ira stating the ill health of Mother; my cold no better.

Dec. 24.

Weather a little moderated and wears very much the appearance of rain. Read 100 lines in Homer's *Iliad* and 150 in Horace. Cold very little better, and spirits very low. Received after dark a serenade of shooting crackers from the few students remaining, as this is Christmas Eve.

Dec. 25th.
Weather cold and dreary; it sleets almost all day. I in the forenoon read 50 lines of Homer's *Iliad*, and in the afternoon write to brother Ira. Health some better, as my cold is beginning to break.

Christmas

Come boys, come one, come all;
Come both ye great and small:
All who can yell and bray,
Celebrate Christmas day.

Bring your fiddle and fife,
And play in merry strife.
The one that'll do the best
Will surpass the rest.

Lay aside all your books:
Richly pay all the cooks,
And let's "old Neddy" sing,
Till the cooks our feast bring.

Look just across the street,
Girls playing in the sleet,
With hearts by no means sad.
Oh! They're stopped by their dad.

How foolish are old folks.
They know nothing of jokes.
The girls wish now to play:
But "stop it" they will say.

But lo! The night has come,
The day has all been spent.
Let's a solemn tune hum,
In prayer be intent.

Let us now meditate,
Why 'tis we celebrate
Christmas in joy and mirth:
Is it some great man's birth?

'Twas then that Christ was born,
Who raised salvation's horn,
A fallen world redeemed,
And on man all truth beamed.

Dec. 26th
Weather somewhat moderated, so that the snow begins to melt. I
study nearly all day. Cold considerably better. Leave Mrs. Hughes,[12]
as she is going on a visit to Cincinnati, and engage boarding at the Oxford Hotel, Mr. Adams proprietor. Society met and discussed with
considerable interest the following question, "Is war ever justifiable?"
It was decided in favor of the Affirmative.

Dec. 27.
Weather warm in comparison to what it has been for the last two
weeks, and on account of the snow melting it is very muddy and disagreeable. I study during the forenoon and after dinner walk about two
miles in the country and spend the whole afternoon in taking recreation. Study after supper until bed time.

Dec. 28.
Weather warm, and it rained nearly all day. I attend church at the New
School Church, Rev. Mr. Tenny officiating, his subject, "The life of
man," and as it is the last sermon of the year 1851, he gave an account
of the progress of the church. My health moderately good.

Dec. 29th.
Weather warm, though wet and dreary. Read 150 lines of Homer's *Iliad*. My health better than usual, as my bad cold is almost entirely well, until about dark when I was attacked with the diarrhea which lasted until the next morning. Mr. Coats from Philadelphia stays all night with me, a student of this place who is a very moral fellow and good student.

Dec. 30th.
Weather very unpleasant as it has rained all day. Read Greek about nine hours. Not entirely over my attack of diarrhea, and from the effects of it I feel very badly, though I hope to get over it without taking any medicine. Begin to be somewhat anxious for school to begin as I am lonesome and low-spirited.

Dec. 31st.
Weather cold and disagreeable. It begins to snow. Complete and review the first book of Homer's *Iliad*. Sat up all the after part of last night with a severe toothache, which is now ceased: my attack of diarrhea renewed last night, so that I now feel very badly, though I shall take no medicine without another relapse.

Charles Elliott was Professor of Greek at Miami during T. C. Hibbett's college years, and lived with his wife in the North Dorm, later named Elliott Hall in his honor. Hibbett was invited to tea with the Elliotts from time to time, and in his senior year he was asked by Prof. Elliott to serve as his sub-librarian.

1852

Jan. 1.
The "new year" came in accompanied by very inclement weather; there is very little excitement. Health very little, if any, better. Study most all day; visit Dr. Huston in the evening and have a very sociable time of it.

Jan. 2nd.
Weather cold and disagreeable, raining and snowing alternately. Saw wood most of the forenoon, as I expect we will soon have some very cold weather again. Read Greek in the afternoon. Society met and discussed the following question, "Was it the best policy for the United States to interfere in the case of Hungary?" It was decided in the Negative. My health is very much better, still convalescent. Read part of *Billy McConnell, The Witch Doctor*, written by Mr. D. Christy of Oxford.

Jan. 3rd.
Weather clear and cold. Return to Mrs. Hughes to board as she came back today. Study all day hard; and retire to bed at 11 o'clock. Health about the same.

Jan. 4th.
Weather clear and exceedingly pleasant, wearing very much the resemblance of spring. Stay in my room all day. Health about the same.

Jan. 5.
The weather has undergone a very material change; instead of being clear and pleasant, it is now on the other extreme, and is now snowing very rapidly. Finish up the second book of Homer's *Iliad*; saw wood enough to do three or four days, as I apprehend the weather will be very cold.

Jan. 6th.
On waking this morning I found that the ground was covered with snow about five or six inches deep and it has snowed all day without

ceasing; and as we have a cold North wind the weather is very unpleasant. Continue reading Homer's *Iliad*. Health very good.

Jan. 7th.
The weather has been extremely cold all day, so much so that it has not snowed any today; the wind has been blowing very rapidly all day, so that the snow is heaped up so that it resembles the billows of the sea during a storm. My roommate E. M. McCartey came back today. I finished the reading of the third book of Homer's *Iliad* this evening, and will, after having reviewed it, recite to Professor Elliott. My health for today is not quite so good as for the few days past, having taken a bad cold on last night, though I hope it will soon be over.

Jan. 8th.
The weather very cold until noon, when after moderating somewhat it commenced snowing and continued until night. Reviewed and recited first three books of Homer's *Iliad*: on examination I passed very creditably. Health tolerably good.

Jan. 9th.
Weather moderately cold though not sufficiently warm to have any effect on the snow. Spend the day in reading Latin, Horace's "Epistola ad Pisones." Health not very good, have a severe pain in my breast: retire to bed early, to try to sleep it off. The debating Society met this afternoon, and discussed the following questions: "Should the fugitive slave law be repealed?": decided in the Negative.[13]

Jan. 10.
Weather moderately cold, and it snowed nearly all day very fast. Continue reading Horace's "Epistola ad Pisones," and finish and review the whole and recite to Professor Moffatt; recitation only passable. Health some though very little better.

Jan. 11.
Weather very cold: the average depth of the snow about 10 inches. Stay in my room all day and read very little. Nearly the whole congregation, which was very large, go to church in sleighs. Health not very good.

Jan. 12.
The weather still cold. Become somewhat uneasy, for fear that something is wrong at home, as I ought to have gotten a letter some two weeks ago. Health no better.

Jan. 13.
The weather extremely cold, as the wind blows fiercely from the North: the sun shines out clearly all day. As my health seems to be getting no better, I resolve to leave off study, so that I may have time to recruit by the time the session takes up, as it is only a week until it will. I finish reading *Old Billy McConnell.*

Jan. 14th.
The weather very much moderated, though not enough to melt the snow in the least. Spent the forenoon in idleness, and in the afternoon I went about four miles in the country to Mr. Lindley's and stayed there until night, and then went to a party at Mr. Ogle's, at which I enjoyed myself very much, but retired to bed early, being very much fatigued from having walked out there, as it was the first time I had walked a distance of any consequence since I left home.

Jan. 15.
Weather quite pleasant in comparison to what it was a few days since: it snowed very rapidly for a while this morning. Return to college this morning in a sleigh. Health moderately good.

Jan. 16.
Weather about the same as yesterday, snowed considerably this morning. Spend the day in idleness pretty much, except writing to brother Ira, as I have become very uneasy for fear that something unusual has happened, as I have not received an answer to a letter written by myself on the 25th of last month. The students are beginning to come in, in crowds. Health tolerably good, somewhat better.

Jan. 17th.
Weather about the same, though in the evening it clouded up as though there would be snow before morning. Visit Professor Moffatt

in the evening. Receive two letters, one from J. F. Bailey, Mt. View, Tennessee, and the other from Robt. Morrison, Jefferson, Tennessee. I am very much rejoiced to hear that Ma's health is no worse. Health tolerable.

Jan. 18th.
Waked up this morning, about half past seven, by the whistling of the wind from the North; it had snowed nearly all night. Keep a good fire and stay by it all day. My health not quite so good on account of the sudden cold change of the weather.

Jan. 19th.
Weather extremely cold, and very clear. Spend the day in making preparations to begin school on the morrow. Health very much improved. Visit Professor Moffatt, and received information that I was promoted by him to the Sophomore Class in Latin.

Jan. 20th.
Weather about the same. School commenced this morning, though not more than 75 present. No recitations today on account of the examinations of new students. Receive a letter from Brother Ira at home. No special news from him. Health good.

Jan. 21st.
On account of the inclemency of the weather, which is as yet very cold, though it has moderated a very little today, our College is as yet quite slim as regards numbers. Some of the classes begin to recite today, though the Sophomore begin tomorrow, as Professors Moffatt and Elliott are still engaged in examinations. Health moderately good.

Jan. 22nd.
This day bore much the resemblance of Spring. I was up before daylight, and to hear the birds so merrily chirping their songs of joy filled my heart with emotions of pleasure indescribable. The sun shone out all day, though not with enough of vigor to have any impression on the snow, which is coated with a hard thick crust. I commenced recitations today and was pretty well prepared on all my lessons. My health is somewhat convalesced. I now retire to bed, it being 11 p.m.

Jan. 23.

The weather today is the same as it was on yesterday. Went through with all my recitations, except in Mathematics, and the omission of this was on account of the absence of Professor Matthews. The hall met this evening and elected the officers for the next term. Have taken a bad cold, from studying with my coat off. I do not feel quite so well as common, on account of which I now retire to bed at 10 p.m.

Jan. 24.

This day bearing so much the resemblance of spring, all nature seems refreshed. The sun shone out warmly all day, so that in the latter part of the day the snow began to melt a very little. I was up and had my fire burning this morning before daylight. First attend Chapel, then a call meeting of the Society, after which I study until noon, when I got a letter from J. L. Cannon, which I answer immediately. My health is not as good as common, as my bad cold has become a great deal worse; I have also the headache. I now retire to bed at 11:30 o'clock.

Jan. 25th.

The sun shining comparatively warmly today, the snow began to melt considerably until nearly night, when it began to change to cold again, and from present appearances it will be snowing before morning. From my ill health last night, I slept very little. I have spent the day pretty much in idleness, except attending preaching in Chapel, the President officiating. Subject: "Lord, what wilt thou have me to do?" I feel some better. Retire to bed at 10 o'clock.

Jan. 26th.

On getting up this morning, to my very agreeable disappointment, I found the weather clear and pleasant, compared with what it was a few days since, though the snow has melted very little today. I attend my recitations regularly and was very well prepared. My bad cold rather worse. Retire to bed at 11 o'clock, though not sleepy.

Jan. 27th.

Get up this morning and have my fire burning before daylight. Our class in German, which recites once per week, commenced recitations this evening to Professor Elliott. The College Temperance Society held a meeting tonight in Chapel; I did not attend. I have been very unwell during the whole day, having the headache together with a bad cold which is no better; although the weather has been truly beautiful, yet I have been in no humor to enjoy it. As I had studied very little all day, and not feeling willing to lose a day at the commencement of a new term, I have studied until twelve o'clock tonight, so that I will be able to attend recitations on tomorrow.

Jan. 28.
This day has passed away in quite a dull manner: first, because it has been cloudy and unreviving, and second, because I have not been in a proper mood to enjoy myself under any circumstances. The snow has melted very fast. Recitations for today passable. My cold is, I think, better: I at least feel better than I did on yesterday. Commence reading Macaulay's history of England,[14] which I think will be very interesting. Go to bed at 10.

Jan. 29th.
The weather has been very pleasant, and I have enjoyed it in some degree. The snow is melting rapidly and the ground is very muddy. My health is somewhat better, though I have a pain in my breast. Go to bed at 10.

Jan. 30th.
The aspect of the weather still bears some resemblance of Spring. Recitations scarcely passable today, as I have not felt much in a studying humor for a few days past. Attend Society meeting, and make an attempt at declamation, though it was a partial failure on account of my embarrassment: was fined for talking to the President without rising. My health very bad and spirits low. The hour is between 12 and 1: not inclined to sleep.

Jan. 31st.
Get up this morning about daylight: on account of not being able to sleep but a very short time, I spent a very restless night. The day has been very dreary, as it has been raining nearly all day. Spend part of the day in looking over Monday's lessons, though have done but little

towards getting them, and the remainder of the day has been spent in lying about. Bad cold gradually wearing off, but the pain in my breast is about the same. My spirits are very low, and I have a most miserable feeling, which is indescribable. Go to bed as early as 9:30 o'clock.

Feb. 1st.

It has changed considerably colder since yesterday, and has been cloudy all day, though it snowed very little. Spend the forenoon in reading, and in the afternoon I attend religious service in chapel, the President officiating. Although the weather was quite inclement, there was a large congregation present, which was very attentive, and behaved in a genteel manner. My health is considerably better than for a few days past, cold entirely well, and breast I think is not in quite so much misery. Retire to bed at 9 o'clock.

Feb. 2nd.

The weather has been cold and unpleasant. Recitations have been pretty good today — I have spent the day in studying pretty hard as my lessons have been more difficult to master, and recite German which is an extra study. Receive a letter from Miss Jane E. Miller at Poplar Grove Academy in Tennessee. As I am 18 years old today, I have commenced a new year of my life. My health has been very much better today than for some time past; in fact I feel almost entirely sound; and in order that I may remain so I go to bed at 10:30 o'clock.

Feb. 3rd.

This has been a very pleasant day; it has moderated very much. Have no recitation to Professor Matthews on account of his ill health. Other recitations were moderately good. I am happy to record that my health is still very good. As all the gas that I have on hand is burnt out I will have to retire to bed, it being about 10 o'clock.

Feb. 4th.

Nothing more than yesterday, everything almost identical except for a great deal of exercise from the effects of which I retire to bed at 10.

Feb. 5th.

The day has been very pleasant until about sunset, when it became cloudy and began to rain, so that it is now becoming much cooler. My recitations for today have been better than usual and I have been very busily engaged at study all day. Received a letter from my friend J. F. Bailey, stating that all the white family at home were well, but several of the Negroes were unwell, though none dangerously ill. My lessons are not quite all prepared for tomorrow, but as I feel quite tired, I resolve to go to bed. My health is, as it has been for several days past, very good. Hour 10:30.

Feb. 6th.
I have spent the day in studying pretty hard as my lessons were unusually difficult. Society met, and the division to which I belong debated the following question. "Should the U.S. interfere against intervention?", which was decided in favor of the affirmative. The weather is quite unpleasant, as it is much cooler and the atmosphere is very damp. Health about the same. As my fire is gone out and I have no more wood sawed, I am forced to go to bed at 12 o'clock.

Feb. 7th.
This was a very pleasant day. The sun shone out brilliantly all day. There is great excitement about Louis Kossuth,[15] and as he will be in Hamilton on Monday the 9th, the two Societies as Societies petitioned the Faculty to grant them permission to go and see him, which was granted willingly. I think that nearly the whole college will go. I however have not the Kossuth fever so strong that I can go. Spend the day in studying partly and partly loafing. Read German at night. Go to bed at 11.

Feb. 8th.
The weather still wears a very charming aspect, so that everything seems full of joy, and from the cheerfulness of nature one could not be otherwise than affected in the same way: so the hours have flown pleasantly and consequently rapidly today. Attended divine service in Chapel this evening, held by Professor Moffatt, and went to church tonight and heard a sermon preached by Rev. Mr. Worrell, the pastor of the Old School Presbyterian Church, and was very well entertained. Health as good as usual. Retire to bed at 9 o'clock as 'tis Sabbath.

Feb. 9th.

The Kossuth fever is still raging very high; the students and citizens talk, comparatively, of no one else; there was no school today as the students, or nearly *all*, went to Hamilton to see him. The inhabitants of Hamilton gave him about 500, accompanied with an address by Mr. Woods of that place. The students did not return until after dark. This has been one of the most lonesome days I have ever spent; I have studied but very little. As the day has been quite pleasant I walked about a great deal, but could find nothing with which to amuse myself. Health still continues to be very good. Retire to bed without knowing my lessons at 10.

Feb. 10th.

The weather today has been very inclement: it has rained almost incessantly all day. I have had only two recitations today on account of the illness of Professor Moffatt. The recitations that I have had, however, were scarcely passable. I have prepared my lessons for tomorrow, and have found time to make, and to put up, my window curtains. I have been well today except for the toothache, which has annoyed me somewhat. Retire to bed at 11.

Feb. 11th.

My toothache had almost ceased last night when I retired to bed, but I was waked up about 1 o'clock this morning with it again and this pain was so severe that I could not rest: so I tried all the remedies of which I had any knowledge, but all was of no effect, and from that till day I was in great pain: so I went this morning to Dr. Huston's office and got him to extract it; it was one of my fore teeth and I was very loath to lose it, but anything rather than pain. I have not studied as diligently today as I should have done and my recitations have been scarcely passable. On account of the loss of sleep which befell me last night, it seems almost an impossibility to study to much advantage tonight. The weather has changed considerably colder, and it has snowed enough to cover the ground and is still snowing. Retire to bed at 10.

Feb. 12th.

After having enjoyed a very refreshing night's sleep I was prepared to enter on today's labors with a much better will than usual. My recitations have all been quite creditable; and by diligent application I have been able to prepare for tomorrow. Retire at 11.

Feb. 13th.
I scarcely know how to begin my minute of today as I do not by any means feel cheerful. My recitations passed off quite creditably: a great deal better than I had anticipated. Society met this evening: my duty being declamation for which I was well prepared, and was complimented for that having been the best attempt that I had made since I have been a member of the Hall. Take a chill, while in the Hall, which lasted about 20 minutes and from the effects of which I as yet feel quite stupid, though I have sat up reading the life of Benjamin Franklin until it is now, I suppose, nearly 12 o'clock. From my melancholy feelings, I have no inclinations towards sleeping, but on account of my fire having gone nearly out, I go to bed.

Feb. 14th. St. Valentine's Day.
The weather has been quite pleasant. There is quite a stir among the students at the post office on account of its being Valentine's day. I have not studied as diligently today as I should have done, the consequence of which is that my lessons are not all prepared for Monday. Health somewhat better. Retire to bed at 10.

Feb. 15th. Sabbath.
The weather has changed very cold and I believe I have scarcely ever known the wind to blow so furiously and steadily for so long a time as it has today; it snowed some once or twice. As I expect to have chill today, and on account of the inclemency of the weather, I did not venture out to church, but have stayed closely by the fire all day. Health no better: I have been very lonesome and melancholy all day, and now retire to rest at 9:30 o'clock.

Feb. 16th.
This day has passed by without anything of great importance transpiring. My recitations have all been very good. On account of the ill health of Professor Matthews we had no recitation in Mathematics. I

have spent the day in close application to my studies; though the sporting of the students on the campus in recreation hours was a great temptation, yet I have withstood it. My health for today, as I am happy to record, is I fancy some better, though I by no means feel well. The day has been cold, though clear and beautiful.

Feb. 17th.

In recording the transactions of this day, I feel as though I will have but a very few more records to make at this place, for unless there is suddenly a very great change in my feelings I will either have to leave here of my own accord or will be called off by the great "I Am," who is omniscient and does all things for the best. I waked, this morning, feeling unusually well, but about 8 o'clock a.m. was taken with the spitting of very black lumps of blood and a violent pain in my breast; this lasted about an hour, after which I seemed to recover and felt very much better until about 5 this evening; then a slight attack of the same returned; although in the last attack I spit comparatively little blood, yet I feel very weak. I as yet have not consulted a Physician, but unless there is a change before morning I think it will be best to do so. I once resolved to write home but I then came to the conclusion that this would not ameliorate my condition, and it would only make my parents uneasy and probably before a letter would reach home I would be well. Go through with all my recitations quite creditably and without saying anything about my illness.

Feb. 18th.

I retired to bed early last night, and had it not been for the horrible dreams that came over me, would have rested quite pleasantly. I did not get up this morning until it was fairly day and my health is very much improved, but I do not by any means feel well. I have not spent the day in very diligent application to my studies, but have walked during the greater part of it, thinking the chief cause of my illness to be on account of not taking sufficient exercise. Attend all my recitations and pass very well. Feeling quite sleepy and very much exhausted, I now retire to bed at 10 o'clock.

Feb. 19th.

After having enjoyed quite a pleasant night's rest (with the exception of an occasional horrible dream) I arose this morning feeling so much better that I fancied myself almost well. My recitations have been nothing more than ordinary, yet better than I had expected. Spend the day in very close application, and as yet am not prepared on tomorrow's lessons. Received a letter from my friend Robt. Morrison, with the perusal of which I was very much delighted. Weather quite pleasant. Now retire to rest at 10 o'clock.

Feb. 20th.

Arose this morning feeling almost entirely well, and as the weather is quite pleasant, my spirits are very much revived. Spend the day very busily, as my lessons had all to be recited by 1:30 p.m. on account of the meeting of the Societies. Attend the Society in the afternoon, but have no duty to perform until evening session, when I took part in debating the following question: "Is a high protective tariff the true policy of the U.S.?", which was discussed with a good deal of interest on both sides. It was decided in favor of the affirmative. I go to bed as soon as I come from Hall at 12.

Feb. 21st.

It has snowed and rained alternately during the whole day, making it very dreary and quite unpleasant; I have studied scarcely any of my lessons except Greek. Write to Robert Morrison. Have an opportunity of attending a party in the country this evening, but decline on account of the inclemency of the weather. Health not so good as for the last two days. Retire to bed at 11:30 o'clock.

Feb. 22nd. Sabbath.

The day has been very dreary as it has rained almost incessantly — I have spent the greater part of the day very unprofitably, not having done anything after Bible recitation, this morning at 8 o'clock. Do not attend church on account of the inclemency of the weather. My health is rather worse as I have been very much annoyed with a severe headache. Receive a good many visits in my room from students. Retire to bed at 9:30 o'clock.

Feb. 23rd.

My recitations for the day have passed very well. I have spent the whole day in close application to my books, as my extra recitation in German came off on this day. Receive a letter from brother Ira, stating that Mother was in very bad health and also, that several of our slaves were sick, and Isham, one of our best slaves, had died a few days before he wrote. From this sad news and the still inclemency of the weather, the state of my health is considerably worse, so just before going to bed I have gone to W. M. Morrison's room and got a dose of Rhubarb. Got to bed at 9:30 o'clock.

Feb. 24th.
I spent last night in a very restless manner without sleeping scarcely any at all. Got up very early this morning and my medicine operated well, after the effects of which I felt very much better. Recitations have all been as good as could be expected. Have spent the day very profitably, though have not prepared all my lessons for tomorrow. This has been the first day this winter which has been warm enough to do without a fire. Attend a lecture this evening at 6:30 o'clock in the Presbyterian Church delivered by Prof. Moffatt, at the request of the students, on the present state of affairs in Europe. The lecture was truly interesting and instructive and from its nature would naturally make attentive ears. Retire to bed at 11:30 o'clock.

Feb. 25th.
After having enjoyed an unusually pleasant night's rest, I awoke this morning quite early and prepared a recitation before Chapel: and have spent the whole day in close application. There has been a great deal of sport on the campus tonight, burning the tall grass, but unfortunately some rude boys fired a private house[16] which brought out the President who ordered all to their rooms.

Feb. 26th.
This, the last Thursday in February, is the regular day for prayer for colleges, and consequently there have been no recitations from 10 a.m. until 4 p.m.; there have been prayer meetings in the different churches in town, and the students, as a college, met tonight for the purpose of prayer. I have done very little studying today and am prepared on none of my recitations for tomorrow. The Faculty have be-

gun to search into the matter of the fire on yesterday evening, saying that those engaged in it will be expelled if found out.

Feb. 27th.

By very close diligence I have been able to get through with my recitations quite creditably today. The students get up a petition requesting the Faculty to overlook the burning of the privy two evenings since, as there were a good many of our best students engaged in it, and as it was done more through thoughtlessness than any real design. Society meet. A communication from the sessional speaker read; he declined. We then elected E. B. Humphrey of Louisville, Kentucky.

Feb. 28th.

This has been one of the dreariest days I have ever spent. It rained incessantly until noon, when it changed cold and the ground froze, so that the falling snow was not melted and tonight it is very clear and cold. To look from my window on the snow, glowing with the silvery rays of a full moon, is truly picturesque, and presents to my mind a natural scene the nearest perfection of any I have yet witnessed. I have spent the day quite unprofitably, scarcely having looked at a book until tonight, since which I have gotten out my Greek. Health good. Retire to bed at 10 o'clock.

Feb. 29th.

Arose quite early this morning, and after taking a bath, I built a fire and dressed and went to breakfast. Attend Bible class from 8 till 9 a.m.; went to preaching in the Methodist Church at 11 a.m. and heard an excellent sermon from Prof. Moffatt, as the regular minister was absent. After getting dinner, I went to sleep and did not wake in time for Chapel services. The day has been quite beautiful. Health good. Retire at 9.

March 1st.

This month came in with the most beautiful weather. Spend the day very profitably; study all day. Recitations all good. Walk about ½ mile during the evening recreation hour. Health tolerably good. Retire to rest at ten o'clock.

March 2nd.

Weather still very pleasant, though not quite warm enough to be entirely without a fire. Spend the day in hard study and my recitations have, all, been passable. Spend ½ hour in recreation by walking. Attend a meeting of the College Temperance Society, held in Chapel this evening at 8 o'clock: the addresses were by Messrs. Steel, Lowrie, and Hibbern. The performance was quite interesting. Retire to bed at 10. Health not good.

March 3rd.

The weather still quite pleasant. Study very diligently all day; and my recitations have all been better than usual. Took an hour's recreation this evening, from the effects of which I feel tired, though not so weary in mind. My health has been much better than it was yesterday. Retire to bed at 10 o'clock.

March 4th.

The weather has been quite disagreeable, it having rained almost incessantly all day and it has also been quite cool. I got up this morning very early, as I had a long lesson to prepare and recite in Mathematics at 8 a.m. I have applied myself very diligently all day, as my lessons have been more difficult, and especially the lesson in Mechanics, consisting of questions to be solved. My health has been moderately good. I feel very much wearied and sleepy: retire to bed at 12:30.

March 5th.

I got up this morning at 5:30 o'clock, after having slept nearly five hours, and was very much hurried until 2 p.m., when my lessons are finished on Fridays. I however knew my lessons somewhat better than usual. Attended the hall this evening, but had no duty to perform as I was to be on debate tonight. There was no meeting of the societies tonight as there was preaching in all the churches in town. Feel well, though sleepy: hour 10.

March 6th.

This day is indeed beautiful. I studied the greater part of the day so that my lessons are nearly all prepared for Monday. Exercise about an hour.

March 7th.

Did not get up this morning until nearly breakfast, this being about 6:30 o'clock. Though the day has been very beautiful, yet I remained in my room during the whole forenoon. Attend divine worship in Chapel this afternoon and heard a sermon preached by N. L. Rice, D.D., from Cincinnati: and I have no hesitancy in saying that he is decidedly the best preacher that I have ever heard, both in beauty of style and deep reasoning. His subject was that man is a free agent. My health is very good. Go to bed at 9:30.

March 8th.

I got up this morning very early and prepared one recitation before Chapel. I have spent the day very profitably, having studied nearly all the time: recitations have been quite creditable. Professor J. C. Moffatt lectured this evening in the Associate Reformed Church on the present state of Hungary; I did not attend on account of pressure of studies. Health good. Retire at 10.

March 9th.

This day has been spent by me in studying very diligently. Learned a declamation for hall. Received a letter from Miss A. Sharp, Benton, Miss. Weather much colder.

March 10th.

This day, although it has been very pleasant, even without any fire, has not been spent by me by any means to the best advantage, not having studied more than ⅔ of the time and the consequence is that I am now to go to bed without knowing my lessons. My recitations today have been good, as they were prepared on yesterday. I hope to get up very early tomorrow morning and make up lost time. Exercised much this afternoon at football. Health tolerably good. Hour 10:30.

March 11th.

I was up this morning much earlier than usual and prepared my lesson in Mathematics before breakfast. I have spent the day in very hard study, though my recitations have not been as good as usual. The weather is truly delightful, it being very pleasant without a fire. My

health has been hardly as good today as usual, owing, I suppose, mostly to close confinement, as I have been too busy to take any exercise at
all today. I had by no means intended, nor have I felt like sitting up until this hour, but my lesson in Mechanics is more difficult than usual.
Hour 12.

March 12th.
I got up this morning very early, though had I consulted my feelings, I
would scarcely have gotten up at all; but the thoughts, that my lessons
were to be *learned* before my recitations would come off, and that the
time for the preparation of which was so short, seemed instinctively to
urge me on to the laborious duty of preparing them. My recitations
today have been better than I had feared they would be. I have spent
the forenoon in close, hard study. In the afternoon I attended Hall
and made a declamation; in making which I was much embarrassed,
though it was gone through as well as I expected. I have given over all
hopes and expectations of ever being an orator, and never expect to
make any pretentions towards eloquence, either of style, or delivery. I
attended Hall also this evening, and listened to the debating of the following questions, "Should the U.S. support a standing army?" The
question was not debated with the usual interest that is commonly
manifested in debates, from the fact that several of the debaters were
unprepared to discuss the question.

March 13th.
This day has been very pleasant, though March quite windy. I attended Chapel this morning and listened to some very good speeches,
after which I occupied myself until noon in writing a letter to Miss
Annie Sharp. In the afternoon I first prepared my Greek lesson for
Monday, and then after taking a walk, sawed wood until I became
quite tired. Feeling very much exhausted tonight I retire to bed very
early. My health much better than it has been for several days.

March 14th. Sabbath.
This day has been quite chilly and the wind has blown very furiously
all day. I attended Bible class at 8 o'clock this morning and have not
been to preaching today; there was no worship in Chapel today except

prayer this morning; the cause of the regular preaching being omitted was that Dr. Anderson is sick and Professor Moffatt has other appointments. I have read some part of Mrs. Herman's poetry this evening which I think very good. I wrote a letter tonight to J. F. Bailey of Tennessee. I do not feel as well tonight as I did yesterday. Go to bed at 10:30.

March 15th.
Begin recitations this week with cheering hopes, in hopes of accomplishing more than I did during the last week. My recitations have all been very good, and though I do not feel very well, yet there is always a pleasant feeling that continues to arise in my breast after having made good recitations. The weather though very windy is quite pleasant. Retire at 10.

March 16th.
I was up this morning very early and went to study. My recitations have been good. As Professor Moffatt was absent, we had only two recitations. I have studied hard all day except an hour's recreation. Health only moderately good. Retire at 11.

March 17th.
The weather has been very disagreeable today, it having rained almost incessantly until about dark, when it changed cold and snowed. My recitations have all been very good, and I have spent the day quite profitably, having studied all day. Health some better, though I feel the want of recreation. Retire to bed at 10.

March 18th.
I got up this morning early and found the ground covered with snow; and from the fierceness of the wind it has been very cold. My recitations for today have not been as creditable as I would like. I have spent the day in close hard study. Health tolerably good.

March 19th.
This day has been very cold and disagreeable. I got up quite early and as usual have been very much hurried, i.e., as usual for Fridays. My

recitations have been scarcely passable. Went to hall this afternoon, but had no performances as I was to take part in debate this evening. Instead of the regular debate this evening, the time was occupied in discussing a resolution, brought up by E. E. Hutcheson and amended by B. Harrison.[17] The discussion lasted several hours, and was conducted with much energy and was at last with a very small majority carried. Retire to bed at 10:30 o'clock.

March 20th.
When I got up this morning I found that it had been snowing: the weather quite cold. Spend the day in preparing Monday's lessons and reading German. Health tolerably good. Received a letter from Miss J. E. Miller.

March 21st.
The weather has somewhat moderated: it snowed considerably this morning, but has since melted away. I attended prayers in Chapel this morning at 8, and Bible recitation at 9, since which time I have been almost idle. I walked about two miles this afternoon, and from its effects feel quite tired. Retire to bed at 9:30.

March 22nd.
The weather has moderated a good deal, though as yet it is quite cool. Recitations today have been very good indeed. I have studied well and took some exercise this evening in the way of jumping. I feel well with the exception of a slight pain in my breast. Go to bed at 10.

March 23rd.
I got up this morning much earlier than usual, as I had a lesson to prepare before Chapel service. I have recited quite poorly, not as well as I knew my lessons by any means. Studied only tolerably well, and have taken no exercise, more than to go to my meals. Attended a call meeting of the Society: having been informed of the non-acceptance of our last elected speaker, we elected another speaker for the commencement exhibition.

March 24th.
As I did not retire to rest last night until 11:30 o'clock, I did not wake

this morning till 'twas quite late. My recitations have been very good. I've studied tolerably well, though I do not know all my lessons for tomorrow. There has been for the last two days great excitement among the students on religion: prayer meetings have been held daily in the college buildings and also at the rooms of the students. The majority of the students attend, and all the attendants manifest much zeal in the cause. It is to be hoped that much good will be done. As I do not feel as well as usual, I retire to bed at 9:30 o'clock.

March 25th.

This day has been quite beautiful, pleasant enough to do without a fire, except for a short time this morning. I have studied but very little, though enough to recite my lessons pretty well. The excitement is still very great. A prayer meeting was held at 6 and one at 8 this forenoon, and since dinner they were held at 1, 4, and 6; and besides, at the different rooms of the students. I feel quite unwell and retire to bed at 9.

March 26th.

There have been no recitations today, as it was thought proper to dispense with college duties on account of the death of Jeremiah Morrow[18], who selected the situation for and founded Miami University, and who has been President of the Board of Trustees since its foundation. There is still great excitement among the students about religion; prayer meetings were held all day either in the college buildings, or at the rooms of the students: the prospect is, that much good will be done. I attended a prayer meeting at the 1st Presbyterian Church tonight. On account of feeling very unwell, I have spent the day principally in walking about. Retire to bed at 10 o'clock.

March 27th.

Met in Chapel this morning at 8 o'clock, and the faculty and students resolved, that, on account of the death of Jeremiah Morrow, all college duties should be dispensed with for two days; and that all should wear the usual badge of mourning for 30 days; after which it was resolved to publish said resolutions. The religious excitement among the students has not been quite so great today, though there have been prayer meetings all day. I attended church tonight.

March 28th. Sabbath.

Met in Chapel at 8 a.m., and after regular chapel service, instead of
Bible recitations as usual, there was a general prayer meeting held in
chapel; and since that there have been prayer meetings all day except
when preaching was going on. I attended preaching in chapel this afternoon at 2 o'clock. We were somewhat disappointed, as we expected
Dr. Rice of Cincinnati to address us, and as he was not there, Dr.
Anderson gave us an extemporaneous address, which was, nevertheless, quite interesting and instructive. I this evening took a walk of
nearly two miles and feel **very, very** tired. Health not good.

March 29th.

There is still great excitement about religion. There was a prayer
meeting held in the Presidential recitation room this morning immediately after Chapel exercises, at the time that my recitation came off
in Mathematics. Besides myself, there was only one more who went to
the recitation; in Latin, there were four present; in Greek, five or six,
and in German we had no recitation at all. I stay closely in my room
and study all day. Health only tolerably good.

March 30th.

As on yesterday, and for the same reason, there were only two present
at recitation in Mathematics; in Latin there were only two present;
and Prof. Moffatt instead of hearing us doubled the lesson for tomorrow; in Mechanics we had no recitation. Prayer meetings are held less
frequently than for a few days past. I attended church this evening and
heard a sermon preached by the Rev. Mr. Davidson of Dayton, an Associate Reformed minister. I think him to be a very eloquent man and
also very sensible. I wrote a letter this afternoon to Miss J. E. Miller. I
feel some better this evening than for a few days past, though on account of the rainy disagreeable weather I feel dull and stupid. Go to
bed at 10.

March 31st.

Recitations still continue to be heard, though from the number of attendants it seems almost like nonsense. The weather is yet very disagreeable, and so cold that I have been obliged to keep a fire all day. I

have taken a good deal of exercise this evening in sawing wood and walking. I feel some little better. Go to bed at 10.

April 1st.

I attended all my recitations regularly, though in most of my classes there were only two present. My recitations were all pretty good, though there was nothing to compel me to attend, as we have now no roll calls, but the very act of staying away would be as much as to say that I was attending prayer meetings; and I can't reconcile it to my conscience to go to prayer meetings merely for the sake of getting clear of recitation. The weather is quite cool and the ground is now covered with snow. Retire to bed at 10:30 o'clock.

April 2nd.

I had no recitation at all today, as Professor Stoddard[19] was absent, having gone to Eaton to attend court. There was not a sufficient number who attended Greek to have a recitation, and as to Latin in the afternoon, there was no recitation on account of the Society being in session at that hour. There was a call meeting of the Society at 9 a.m., and we resolved to meet this afternoon at 1, so as to get through by 3 in order to go to church at that hour, as Dr. Rice of Cincinnati was to preach. Health only tolerably good.

April 3rd and 4th.

Fortunately I neglected to have the letter mailed which I wrote to brother Ira on the 3rd. I was taken on the evening of the 3rd with a violent chill which lasted about three hours, after which a violent fever seized me, after suffering with which for two hours I fell into a perspiration and it passed off with a very violent headache. I have during my life had several chills, but this I'm forced to record as the most violent; it seemed as though my back would certainly be dislocated from the great aching which I suffered. I was all alone as all were attending church. I slept but very little that night. I have stayed in my room all day (this the 4th) and feel much better; in fact, well, except for a slight headache, and my back has not gotten well. I took a dose of antibilious pills this evening according to the advice of the doctor. I retire to bed early. Weather very wet and quite cool, which renders it very disagree-

able, though I ventured to my boarding house at 12 to get something
to eat.

April 5th.
I did not get up this morning until it was quite late; being very unwell
from my medicine, I did not go to breakfast or Chapel service. My
medicine kept me sick till about noon, when after eating but a little
dinner I felt much better. I did not attend any recitation. The weather
is still damp and cool.

April 6th.
I was up this morning very early, and though very weak, yet feel better
than I have for some time past. I wrote a letter to John F. Bailey so
that they might know at home how I was getting along. I did not
attend any of my recitation, but occupied the day in reading, preparing tomorrow's lessons, and exercise. The weather has become much
more pleasant, though somewhat cool. Retire to bed at 9 o'clock.

April 7th.
This day has been very beautiful indeed; and I was up quite early and
had all my lessons prepared by the time they were to be recited. My
health is very good, yet I feel quite weak when I attempt the least exer-
tion. Go to bed very early.

April 8th.
This day has not been spent so profitably as it might have been. I went
through with all my recitations very creditably, but tomorrow's lessons
have not been very well prepared. The weather is still very beautiful,
though too cool to be entirely without a fire, and with my present good
health, I can't but feel happy and be sensible of the blessings with
which at this time it seems that God is especially favoring me.

April 9th.
I, this morning, got up very early and was able, by making a good start,
to get through with all my recitations very creditably. I attended hall
this afternoon. The business before the house was to pass some resolutions which were discussed at a previous meeting. There was a very

warm debate, in which many enemies were made and a few friends. Accusations of belonging to factions were alleged, and secret Societies exposed.[20] Although I did not allow myself to participate in the debate, yet I became quite angry. We adjourned to meet next Friday as there is preaching in the churches this evening.

April 10th.
This day has been very unpleasant, it having rained almost incessantly all day, and in addition to this it has been quite cool. During the forenoon, after having attended the regular Saturday's exercise in Chapel, I wrote a letter to cousin Alfred H. Sharp. During the afternoon I have employed myself in preparing Monday's lessons and reading German. Retire to bed quite early.

April 11th. Sabbath.
I have stayed in my room nearly all the time today, except to hear preaching in the New School Presbyterian Church under the charge of the Rev. Tenny; the sermon was quite interesting and instructive. Weather has been quite cool and disagreeable. Health only moderately good.

April 12th.
I have been in a great deal of misery today with a crick in my neck, so that it is with great pain that I can move my head at all. I attended all my recitations, and passed very well considering my bad feelings. The weather has not been quite so cool today, but very disagreeable on account of the rain.

April 13th.
I was up this morning very early, but from the crick in my neck, which is no better, I have not passed the day with much pleasure, though I did not fail to attend my recitations. The day has been truly beautiful, though too cool to be entirely without a fire. Retire early.

April 14th and 15th.
I have nothing of any consequence to record for these two days, and that I may make my daily records somewhat interesting, I have re-

solved, that when a day passes off without anything unusual having happened, I will defer making my record until the following evening, and bring them both under one, and thus avoid making, as much as possible, (as the saying is) a stereotyped affair of it, though it is impossible to avoid this entirely, for at college we have our regular business to go through with and have little time for anything else. The weather has become very beautiful. My health is better.

April 16th.
As usual on Fridays, this has been quite a busy day. Two of my recitations were very good and the other was a complete failure. The Society met this evening; there were very few present, from some unknown cause. My performance was composition. In the evening session, as there were very few present, we all joined in the debate and had a very interesting time of it, as all became interested: the question was "Should capital punishment be abolished?"

April 17th.
After the regular Saturday's exercise in Chapel, viz., orations and composition, which were much more interesting than usual, I got out my Greek lesson before dinner, and after dinner I first took a game at marbles (which has become very common) and then went to work at my mathematical lesson. I retire to rest quite early feeling very well.

April 18th.
This day has been very beautiful. I attended Bible class this morning at 8 to Prof. Elliott, and have been to church twice. I took a short walk this evening, it being the first for some time, and am quite tired.

April 19th and 20th.
These days have been very cool, almost like winter. I have done more than my usual amount of study, but seem not to get along so well in my classes. I attended a lecture tonight in the town hall over the market house; the subject of the lecture was to prove that slavery was an evil *per se* and should therefore be abolished. There were very few arguments brought up, and what *were* brought up were handled by no means to the best advantage. There was a great crowd of negroes pres-

ent, and from their almost incessant cheering, it was very annoying, both to the speaker and the respectable portion of the auditors; the crowd very much resembled a mob. Retire to bed very late.

April 21st and 22nd.
The weather still wears a very gloomy aspect; it is quite cool; the ground froze last night. I wrote to my friend J. F. Bailey today in order that they might hear at home how I am getting along. My health has been moderately good. Got excused from Chapel performance. Recitations only tolerably good. Sit up tonight until 11 o'clock.

April 23rd.
As is by no means extraordinary of Fridays, this has been a very busy day. I attended all my recitations regularly, which were all perfect according to grade. In the afternoon attended hall and listened to some very good compositions and declamations. In the evening session we debated the following question, "Is a man morally bound to marry?" The question was very ably debated, and unexpectedly no indecencies were indulged in, with improper motives; all were much interested and broke up in perfect good humor. The great excitement about "Secret Societies" is almost entirely abated, and we are beginning to be united again as a band of brothers. Retire to bed, very much exhausted, at 11:30, with hopes of having a good night's rest.

April 24th and 25th.
I studied my Monday's lessons the greater part of the day and the remainder was occupied in reading a portion of Sidney Smith's lectures on Moral Philosophy. Sabbath, I went to church twice, once to the Old School and once to the New School Presbyterian Church; four of my intimate friends joined the Old School church. Weather very wet and cool.

April 26th and 27th.
My recitations for these two days have been very much worse than usual, though not for any lack of the proper amount of study being bestowed on them, but because I have not been in the proper condition to retain what I've studied. My health has been only moderately good;

I have felt quite dull, and as though I were forced to sustain some preponderous load. I had a long talk with a Phi [Delta Theta] today; he was trying to persuade me to join said Society immediately. I declined, on the grounds that I preferred, for the present under existing circumstances, to be entirely free from all restraints of Secret Societies.

April 28th and 29th.
The weather for these two days has been very much more pleasant. I have studied very hard and graded above 95, 100 being perfect. Visited my friends McLean and Ross; had quite a pleasant time. There was a hail storm this evening; though the hail stones were very large, yet there was very little damage done, as it continued but a short time. Retire at 11 o'clock.

April 30.
As is very unusual for Fridays, I got through with my recitations quite easily, having been able to partially prepare them yesterday. The Society met this evening, and the regular business was dispensed with, as there was a new constitution to be laid before the Society for reception or rejection; it was carried in toto; the question about having the meetings of the Society opened with prayer arose, and there was quite an exciting time; it was decided, on vote, in the affirmative; the Society will, then, hereafter be opened with prayer. After the reception of the new constitution, there was an election of officers: all the officers elected were Alphas or Betas,[21] i.e., all of any importance; no opposition was made by their opposers the Phis; they, however, by no means consider themselves very materially injured, especially when they take in consideration who are their opposers. I feel quite weary, and have a very severe pain in my left lung. Retire at 11.

May 1st and 2nd.
There was expected to be a great May party on the first, but on account of there being sacramental meetings in the churches, it was postponed. I studied quite faithfully on that day and prepared all my Monday's lessons. After night I went to a secret meeting of Phis in order to consider the past, and make future preparations for any such

emergencies in reference to the way we had been secretly and wrong-
fully abused, in order that some others might hold sway in the Hall.
Come in at 12. On Sabbath I attended Bible class at 8 a.m. and also
church at 11. In the afternoon at 3, I attended church again in Chapel,
where Prof. Moffatt preached a very good extemporaneous sermon.
The weather has been somewhat cool, though not very unpleasant. I
slept very little on Saturday night, on account of going to bed late (as
above said) and I have been troubled considerably with a severe pain
in my left lung; this however is better, and with this exception I have
enjoyed my usual health.

May 3rd and 4th.
Monday, I got along, as to lessons, very well, but Tuesday's were miser-
ably gotten over. Prof. Elliott left this morning, as his health has become very bad; he will probably not come back until next session.
Prof. Bishop takes his place, and Mr. Chambers takes Prof. Bishop's
place in the Preparatory Department. I like very much to recite to
Prof. Bishop, as he is very particular that we have everything perfect. I
wrote a letter to Pa today and handed it to M. M. Wilson to deliver, as
he is to start to Tennessee tomorrow to teach school and expects to be
in our neighborhood. Health has been only moderately good.

May 5th and 6th.
I have been getting along quite poorly since my last record was made,
owing principally, I suppose, to my health having become worse. I
can't say that there is anything particularly the matter, but I feel very
weak from close confinement, scarcely having been out of sight of the
college since my arrival at this place, some 10 months since. There is a
concert going on in town tonight; instead of going, I have stayed in my
room and read German.

May 7th.
Sophomore class have not had a recitation today; in the forenoon nearly all went to the concert in town and the remainder did not go to recitation; in the afternoon Prof. Moffatt was absent. Society met at the
usual hour of meeting; in the reception of the minutes of last meeting,
Mr. E. E. Hutcheson moved that all the part relating to the election of

officers be stricken out, on the ground that it was unconstitutional to have an election of officers merely because an amendment was made to the Constitution, as the new Constitution was offered as an amendment to the Old. The yeas and nays were called for, and it was carried by a very small majority that the minutes should remain as they were. During the evening session, the following question was debated, "Should the US pass a law regulating the interest on loans?", in which I was a participant. There was a petition sent in to the faculty requesting them to give the whole of tomorrow as holiday, which they granted. Weather quite pleasant.

May 8th and 9th.
As we had no college duties to perform today, I have had sufficient time to prepare all my lessons, and as the day was quite pleasant, took considerable exercise. On Sabbath during the forenoon I occupied myself in reading, and after dinner, as I felt quite unwell, I lay down to take a sleep and did not wake until after preaching was over in chapel. Feel well, except at times I am very much troubled with a pain in my left lung. Retire early.

May 10th and 11th.
I was up very early, and though I felt very unwell, I went through all my recitations very creditably. Took a long walk in the evening and by the time I got back, I was very weary and quite sick at the stomach, so that I was forced to go to bed. This morning, the 11th, I was up early, but by no means have gotten over yesterday's walk. I attended all my recitations except to Prof. Stoddard. It has been raining all day. I have occupied a considerable time in reading German. Retire at 10:30.

May 12th and 13th.
I have been getting along quite poorly for these two days. Recitations have been badly, for the most part, recited. Health has been rather on the decline; my greatest trouble is a soreness about my breast. I have made it a rule to walk about one mile every evening between supper time and dark, though it wearies me very much. I went in swimming this evening as the weather is getting warm. I have almost quit studying all night and go to bed at 9 o'clock.

May 14th and 15th.

During this day (the 14th), I've gotten on very much better than usual in every respect; the day has been somewhat unpleasant, on account of its being quite cool. I attended hall this evening, and our exercises were better than usual in the composition and declamation line, as the senior Phis went it pretty strong in their defense in that way. I requested to leave the hall, but by the request of friends, consented to stay. Debate was whether common schools should be supported by taxation. Saturday studied well. Health much better.

May 16th.

As the day has been very pleasant and cheering, I have enjoyed myself quite well. During the forenoon, after attending Bible class, I have occupied my time in reading. In the afternoon, after attending church in chapel, I have been walking until dark, soon after which time, feeling quite tired, I retire to bed. I have felt moderately well.

May 17th and 18th.

These days have been spent very profitably. The weather has been almost too cool to be without a fire and yet very fair. My health has been very good, i.e., very much better. I took a long walk with my friend Theophilus McLean this evening, after which we retired to Clute's[22] and had some ice cream and lemonade.

May 19th and 20th.

Since my last record, the weather has been so cold that we have been compelled to keep a fire all the time. Commenced review. 20th: Senior examination commenced today. Read a part of Byron's works. Took a long walk this morning.

May 21st.

The weather somewhat, though very little, moderated. Recitations very poor. Attend hall for irregular business, as, under the new constitution, we are only required to attend every two weeks. I left after irregular business was over. Our Sessional speakers were elected, viz., E. E. Hutcheson, Joseph McNutt, J. H. Brooks, W. S. McNair, Jas. W. Steel. During the evening session the debate went off quite poorly.

May 22nd and 23rd.

Rained all day, making it too disagreeable to be out of my room, so I built a fire and studied my lessons until noon, after which read portions of Dean Swift's poetry. Sabbath, attend Bible class from 8 to 9 a.m. and read Greek Testament until dinner, after which read *Childe Harold* by Lord G. G. Byron.

May 24th and 25th.

Weather warmer, though rainy and disagreeable. Get through recitations much better than usual. Much disorder in my room this evening: which, by my attempts to stop it, I fear, has been the cause of a loss of some of my best friends, as I became quite angry and used some very rough expressions. Health not so good, retire to bed at 10 o'clock.

May 26th and 27th.

I have gotten through these two days and have enjoyed myself but very little; in the first place my health has been bad, and in the second place, my lessons have been much longer and more frequent, and as the Profs have come to the conclusion that we will not get through with as much as was expected unless they go on with such an arrangement. The weather has become much warmer. Our Catalogues for this year came up today from Cincinnati. Received a letter from Miss J. E. Miller and answered it. There was a great row started on the Campus tonight, something like a mock serenade, with drums, tin pans, fifes, etc., but the President soon appeared, and such a scatterment has not been among the boys in modern times. Do not retire to bed until after 12.

May 28th.

Weather warm. Society met this afternoon. Performance went off without much variety. Evening session we met, but the majority of the members were in favor of adjournment. But a few of us stayed and had a general debate.

May 29th and 30th.

Saturday was too warm for comfort. I stuck pretty close to my books, but it seemed as though I could not concentrate my thoughts to my

subject enough to acquire much knowledge of it. Obtained permission
from the President to go home a week or two before the close of the
session. As the permit was rather unexpected and I had thought nothing about it, I was unprepared to say whether I would avail myself of
the opportunity or not. I rather think I'll stay here until after Commencement is over. Sabbath, attend Bible class, and in the afternoon,
preaching in the Chapel. Read some in the Greek Testament, and also
a portion of Adler's *German Reader*. I have not been very well, occasioned mostly by eating too much, as I have an almost ungovernable
appetite. Took a long walk this evening via Main Street as the weather
was very pleasant and I now feel weak and tired. Occupied myself tonight until 10 o'clock in meditation and reading German.

May 31st.
Receive a letter from Pa in which was enclosed $20 Tennessee money.
His advice was for me to return home through Kentucky, as the cholera is beginning to break out on the river. The measles are beginning
to break out in our family. I answer the letter this afternoon. The Junior Class have gotten up a petition today praying the faculty to exam-
ine their class next after the Grammar School; and the Sophomores
and Freshmen are getting up a remonstrance against it, which they
will send in to the faculty at the same time that the Juniors send in
their petition.

June 1st and 2nd.
Owing to the weather being very warm, I have not studied so well as I
should have done, and of course my recitations have not been so good
as they might have been. Visit Prof. Bishop and draw $20, which I paid
Mrs. Hughes on her account against me for board. We had a long lecture this morning in Chapel from Dr. Anderson on account of the
noise and frolicking on the Campus last night until after midnight.
Nearly every fellow in college has gotten up some kind of a badge in
order to burlesque the Secret Societies.

June 3rd and 4th.
Since the rain which fell on the night of the 2nd, the weather has been
much cooler. On the 3rd nothing happened worth relating. On the 4th

we finished *Aeschines de Corona* [a Greek oration by Demosthenes], and will commence review on Monday. In the afternoon the Hall met. I offered the following resolution, viz., Resolved, that while one division of the Society is in session, no member of the other division has a right to make or second a motion to adjourn, or vote on such a motion when made. I was not allowed to speak on it, as the President decided that it was not a resolution but a By-Law, and as such "would have to lie on the table two weeks and be read three times before adoption," and then would be the proper time for debating. I refused to offer it as a By-Law as we would only have two more meetings this session. Mr. E. E. Hutcheson made a motion to amend our Constitution by putting in its stead the first Constitution the hall ever had; it carried, and the Constitution read the first time was laid on the table. No meeting this evening as there was preaching in town.

June 5th and 6th.
Spend Saturday the 5th very unprofitably, not having done scarcely anything except to read a part of Ike Marvel's "Dream Life." Secret Society met this evening (i.e., Kappa Gamma Theta, which is a burlesque on the Secret Societies in College). Mr. R. C. Lewis having been called to the chair, I, together with E. E. Hutcheson and Seabury Hunt, was appointed to draft a constitution, which I have been at this evening. Nearly all the other Secret Societies, which were gotten up for a burlesque, have died away; ours has had the desired effect: at least all the real ones have taken off their pins and yielded the day. The Phi Delta Thetas have been caucusing, for the purpose of concerting means wherewith to have a call meeting of the Miami Union Literary Society, for the purpose of initiating the officers to be elected at the last meeting of the Society if the new constitution carries — as they do not wish to have their diplomas signed by Mr. Chambers, who is now President and an Alpha Delta Phi. Sunday, the 6th, attend church once, and went to sleep this afternoon and even lost my supper. The weather is and has been for two days too cool to be without a fire. Health moderately good.

June 7th and 8th.
The weather has been very cool and wet so that we have been obliged

to keep up fires. As I am now reviewing and the Professors (as is very unusual in review) do not make our lessons **very** much longer than the first time going over, we have much easier times than I had feared we would have. I have occupied the most of my time in writing a constitution for the Kappa Gamma Theta Society, and reading German. On invitation I called to see Prof. Trimbly this evening and had quite a pleasant time. Health has been very good.

June 9th and 10th.
The weather still quite cool. John Lindly[23] left today to go to our neighborhood. I did not get to see him after I heard he was going or I would have gone with him. I heard today that the measles were getting very bad at home, and I shall be uneasy until I hear from there. The Kappa Gamma Theta Society met last night, for the purpose of ar-raigning one of the members for some trifling offense, for which we fined him a treat for the Society. We had a grand time and there were good speeches made on both sides. Did not get to bed till after 12 o'clock.

June 11th and 12th.
These days have been very dreary and spent quite unprofitably. I have almost entirely quit studying. This morning I got up with the diarrhea, but it soon stopped itself. I did not attend hall on this account. I understand however there was no particular business transacted. The regular business was not permitted to come off, and the other division adjourned us as soon as regular business was over, through want of some rule to prevent such an unfairness. Saturday I loafed nearly all day after reading over my Greek.

June 13th. Sabbath.
Ran off from Bible class this morning; from that till dinner I sewed buttons on my shirt and packed up the most of my clothes so as to begin to prepare to go home. This afternoon I attended the funeral of Prof. Moffatt's brother at his house; the funeral was preached by Dr. Anderson. The procession was about 300 yards long, which followed the corpse on foot to the college graveyard, where after quite an appropriate prayer from Dr. Scott[24] he was buried. The weather changed much warmer. Health moderately good. Go to bed at 10:30.

June 14th and 15th.

These being the last two study days of this collegiate year, very little
has been accomplished in the way of study, as our lessons have been
too long for us to have time to possibly look over them. A great deal of
sport is carried on at night on the campus, and it is only a very few
hours before daylight that there is a possibility to sleep anywhere
about the college from the noise. Received a letter from J. F. Bailey informing me that the measles were getting better at home, and the
cholera was breaking out in the neighborhood. Weather warm.

June 16th and 17th.

The weather has been so excessively warm that times have been very
dull. We had no recitations today (except a general review of our
Mathematics), on account of the examinations of the students in the
Preparatory Department, which took place today. 17th: The Sopho-
mores were examined in Mathematics: all passed respectably well.
Frolicking on the campus still kept up at night. I have begun to read
Pollack's *Course of Time.*

June 18th and 19th.

Time is beginning to hang very heavy. I determined today to start for
home on Wednesday the 24th, so as to take a regular packet from
Cincinnati to Nashville, as there is only one per week; I believe I had
rather miss commencement than have to stay here a week after the
session is out, especially when all the boys will be gone home. We were
examined in Greek today; pass very well. 19th: Pack up my trunk, and
deposit the greater part of my books in Mr. Morrison's room, as they
will be safer there than in my own. Review part of my Mechanics this
afternoon, as I fear we will stand a poor examination in it. Attend an
address before the Junto Society this evening, in the Old School Presbyterian Church, by E. E. Hutcheson. The audience was very large,
and the address very appropriate and about 1½ hours long. I slept
very little last night as I was troubled very much with a pain in my
breast, which has now entirely ceased, but from want of sleep and ex-
haustion I feel very bad; and though it is now only 10:30 o'clock, I retire to bed, hoping to be refreshed by a good night's rest. So good
night.

June 20th and 21st. Sabbath.

Owing to my bad health, I stayed in my room nearly all day, though the temptation was very strong for taking me to church, as Dr. Anderson delivered his Baccalaureate today before the present Senior class. The house was crowded. The Rev. Davidson of Hamilton, Ohio, delivered an address, this evening, before the Society of Inquiry, in the First Presbyterian Church; the audience could not by any means get in the house. It is reported to have been a grand speech. Monday, June 21st. I feel somewhat better than yesterday. Our examination took place in Latin at 10 a.m.; all got through well; we were examined this afternoon in Mechanics; we passed much more easily than any of us expected. The weather has been exceedingly warm and uncomfortable.

June 22nd.

Health about the same. Spend the day in making preparation to go home, i.e., paying off my bills. Great preparations are being made for commencement; I am tempted to stay, and were it not for the cholera getting worse on the river I would.

June 23rd.

I was up at 4 o'clock so as to be ready for the stage and carried my trunk over to Mrs. Hughes', as that was the place the agent agreed to instruct the driver of the Omnibus to call for me, but he forgot to tell him, and I was left; so I went to the Livery stable and hired a horse and buggy, and Mr. Brown went with me to Hamilton about 9 a.m., and took the cars from that place to Cincinnati; when I got to the depot, the Omnibus driver, in a great hurry, took my trunk and left me, and I thought I had seen my trunk for the last time. I hired an Omnibus and went to the Broadway Hotel, and after about an hour's search found my trunk. My next business was to find a boat going to Nashville, but there was not one on the wharf that would start before the next evening; as the weather was quite cool, and it had been raining all day and was very wet, I began to get sick of my trip and wished I had waited till some of the college boys were coming down this way. Made arrangements with the clerk on the boat *Jenny Lind* to take me to Nashville for $10, and went on board at 2 o'clock p.m., where I

thought I'd be better satisfied than at the tavern, but soon found that
there was no one else on board but the deck hands and they were
loading the boat. I got along pretty well until night when the Captain
came to me and introduced me to a fellow, who was to take the upper
berth in my room. I was much pleased with this at first, for I was really
afraid to stay on board by myself, as I had no lock on my door nor any
way to fasten it; but with a very little conversation with my roommate I
found he was a regular "Black Leg," and he used every means, first to
get me to drink a little, as the weather was wet and cold, but this I pos-
itively refused under pretense of being a Son of Temperance. He then
tried to get me to play a game of Euchre "just for fun and to pass off
the time." I told him I did not know how to play and did not wish to
learn. He then, after getting pretty drunk, retired to bed. I tried my
best to keep from sleep, but couldn't, and slept sound all night, except
for being waked once by someone leaving my room, but fortunately I
had put my pocket-book down my drawer leg, which I thought would
be safer than under my pillow. Health has been moderately good.

June 24th.
Got up very early, and as the sun shone out clearly I was much
cheered, and walked about on the wharf so as to amuse myself. I was
very uneasy all day for fear the boat would be there another day, but
fortunately we got off about 6 o'clock p.m. I took supper at seven. Go
to bed at 8. Wind blowing very strong from the West. The boat shakes
so I can scarcely write.

June 25th.
Waked this morning and found the boat tied up at Madison, which
from the river seemed as though it was a very beautiful and healthy little place, situated on the Indiana side of the river. Arrived at Louisville
at 9 a.m. and left at 2 p.m. Hired a pilot to take us over the shoals, as
the water is very low, and pass New Albany about 3 p.m. Retire to bed
early.

June 26th.
Waked this morning very early and found the boat had been tied up
nearly all night on account of the fog, which was so thick one could

scarcely see his hand before him. Started about 7 a.m. and had not
gone far before we had to go ashore and fix the pumps, which were out
of order: so we did not get fairly under headway until 9 a.m. We have
stopped at several villages today, the names of which I do not know.
The nights are cold and towards the middle of the day it is very warm.
Feel quite unwell this evening and go to bed before dark, and leave
quite a merry crowd in the cabin.

June 27th.
Got up this morning about daylight, as I could not imagine why the
boat was lying still; after being dressed and going out on deck, I found
that on account of the fog last night she had run on a sand bar. She was
soon helped off and we put out again. Amuse myself with walking
about on the Hurricane deck until the sun got too warm. Arrived at
Smithland at 9 a.m. and took in a good many passengers. This place is
small and of very little importance when compared with what I expected to find it. Stay at it about an hour. Start up Cumberland River,
which looks like a little branch by the side of the Ohio. Met a boat at
Eddyville, and learned that it would be an impossibility for our boat to
go much farther up the river, as the water in several places was only
about 18 inches deep, and our boat could not go without any load; of
course, we were all very sorry to hear this news, as we then saw no way
of getting up for a week by river, and the stage did not start out for
three days. Our captain gave orders for the boat to be unloaded, which
kept them until 12 o'clock at night. I did not go to bed till 2 the next
morning, looking for a boat to come along and take us. The mosquitoes were as thick as a swarm of bees.

June 28th.
Our boat started up the river very early to get the loading off a boat
which was hung on a rock; arrived at Canton at about 10 a.m., where
we were put on shore, and our boat attempted to go on up the river
about a mile, where this other boat was hung, but could not get there,
and they started back to Cincinnati. Hire a boy to take our trunks to
the Canton Inn, where we learned that the stage was to leave from
that place for Nashville the next morning at 11 a.m. We then concluded to go by stage, as they told us it was uncertain whether a boat

would be along for Nashville in a week or not. Weather wet and dreary. The town scarcely deserved the name of such, and what few people were there, seemed as though they were very little above heathen in point of civility. I scarcely know at what to occupy myself. Employ a boy to watch the river and let us know in case there should be a boat passing up. Go to bed at dark.

We were waked up this morning at 1 o'clock with the news of a boat coming, which all rejoiced to hear. The boat stopped on account of the fog, and by 2 o'clock we were all on board; found the boat crowded, as they had been taking in passengers from the mouth of the Cumberland up; as there was no place to sleep, we sat up the remainder of the night. Start up the river about sunrise. We traveled all day at the rate of about two miles per hour, and stopped about every five miles to take in or let out passengers, though there were very few who went out. Pass one boat which had sunk, one hanging on a rock and could not get off, and another which could not go either up or down. We took all their passengers, who were willing to take deck passage on our boat rather than be left. As the weather was excessively hot, and having nothing to drink except river water, and nothing fit to eat (for the cabin stunk so, I came near vomiting), I feel quite unwell, sleepy and very tired; but as there was no place to lie down, I contented myself with sitting up and fighting the mosquitoes, which were very annoying. Pass a boat which had just burned up. All were saved. I never spent a longer night in my life.

June 30th.
I have been too unwell today to notice much that passed. Weather still **very** warm. From the time we left Clarksville yesterday evening, we have averaged two miles per hour, coming over the shoals; after having tried two or three times and failing, the hands waded the river and pulled the boat up by ropes. Get in sight of Nashville at 2, but it took us two or three hours to pass a little island just below the place. As soon as we landed, I went around to see whether the cars had gone out, and found they had been gone 15 minutes. Have my trunk taken to the Inn, and walk around town to see whether any of our folks were in town or not, but finding none, I went up and looked at the capitol

and then went round and saw where James K. Polk[25] was buried. Then go to supper. Retire to bed before dark, but on account of the warmth of my room did not get to sleep until about 10 o'clock.

July 1st.

I was waked this morning at 5 o'clock, but feeling unwell I did not take breakfast. Got in a hack[26] to go to the cars at 6 o'clock, but as the driver wished to get a load we drove around town till nearly 7. When I arrived at the depot there was such a crowd, all trying to be attended to first, that I was afraid I would not get my trunk on at all, so I hired a boy to rush mine in or knock somebody down; we got out to Lavergne[27] at about 8 a.m. I carried my trunk to Buchanan's shop and walked down home. All seemed glad to see me. I found several sick with the measles.

Aug. 24th.

As I was for the most part idle, and it being frequently inconvenient on account of my not being at home, I have not kept my journal during this vacation. And another thing is, there has been so little to give variety to my records, that I think it would not have been practicable. The first week or two were spent in going to see my former schoolmates and acquaintances, who, I flatter myself, were all pleased to see me. I then visited Uncle D. C. Hibbett's in Wilson County, thence to Uncle John Hibbett's in Sumner County, where I saw my aged grandmother, now in her 84th year; she enjoys good health and looks as though she might live 10 years longer as to physical strength. After I came back home and had become rested from my trip, I was taken with the flux, but said nothing about it for nearly a week, hoping that it would soon wear off, but I found that instead of wearing off it was daily growing worse. The Doctor was called in and in a few days he stopped the bleeding, but left me so weak I was scarcely able to walk. My health gradually improved until this evening, when I thought I was able to stand a trip back to Oxford, though my father and mother were both very loath to permit me to leave without being entirely well. But under the consideration that I would barely get to College in time to begin with my class, they finally submitted. After getting my trunk packed with the clothes which my mother had prepared for me, and eating my supper, I set out at 5 o'clock p.m. for the cars, where I met Mr. Morrison who would accompany me. Got on the cars at Lavergne and had quite a pleasant trip to Nashville, where we arrived about dark. After seeing my trunk safe at the tavern, I went to the stage office and engaged my passage to Louisville, after which I accidentally met with the Rev. Wm. T. Buell, who conducted me to the Rev. D. Edgars, where I met Mrs. Buell; after sitting an hour and eating some ice cream, I took leave of them and went back to the tavern. Retire to bed at half after eleven, very much exhausted.

Aug. 25.
Was waked by the tavern keeper at a little before 3 with the news that the stage was waiting for me. I got up and prepared to go, but I felt very much like going towards home, when such a tiresome journey stared me in the face. My bowels pained me very much, but after getting a good draught of brandy, they seemed very much relieved, and I set out on my journey quite much encouraged. After having gone about 25 miles, we stopped for breakfast, but as I felt unwell I declined eating. We took dinner at about 12 o'clock. I ate quite heartily, as this was the first since I left home. After getting a good drink of ice water, we were off again; towards evening I became very weary; my bowels pained me very severely, and when we stopped in Bowling Green for supper, I felt as though I could go no farther, but after drinking some brandy and two large cups of strong coffee, I felt much better, and got on well.

Aug. 26.
Arrived at Bell's tavern, opposite the Mammoth Cave, this morning at one o'clock; here we found 10 new passengers who wished to go to Louisville, so we put on as many as would cover the top and set out on a dirt road. This was rather a trying time on our patience, as the roads were very muddy on account of the late heavy rains, and with a heavy load we were compelled to go very slow. The night was dark and quite cool. Came to Greene River at 2 o'clock, where, dark as it was, we had to walk a long hill on each side of the river. When I got to the top I was completely exhausted. Took breakfast at 8. Weather very warm. Took dinner at 4 and had nothing fit to eat. From the tavern we walked

down to Salt River and up a long hill on the opposite side. We arrived in Louisville at 9. Being very much exhausted, I did not wait for supper, but went immediately to bed.

Aug. 27.

After having enjoyed quite a refreshing night's rest, I got up at 5 o'clock, ate a very hearty breakfast at 6, and walked about town until 8, then went to the river and engaged my passage to Cincinnati on the *G. W. Sparhawk;* had my trunk brought down and we were off at 10 a.m. As I felt comparatively almost well, I enjoyed myself very much.

Aug. 28.

Waked this morning at 5, and found our boat landed at the Cincinnati wharf. Bought a ticket for the cars, and without getting my breakfast, hired a hack to take me to the railroad depot, where I arrived at 7; in a few minutes we were off for Hamilton; reached Hamilton at 8, and at 9 we set out by stage for Oxford. Met several of my schoolmates in Cincinnati and some in Hamilton. We were all glad to see each other. At 1 o'clock p.m. I was in my room, where I met my roommate.

Aug. 29th.

I was up quite early this morning and feel somewhat rested from my fatigue of traveling. The first thing after breakfast was to redeem the promise I made to my father when I left home, i.e., to write to him so soon as I should arrive at Oxford. The remainder of the day was spent in visiting my old schoolmates. I had intended to have gone to Church tonight, but one of my particular friends called on me, and I was prevented.

Aug. 30th.

This morning we had Chapel meeting for the first time this year. Nothing was done in College except the examination of new students, of whom there were 65 present. Bought what books I would use this session and arranged my library with what books I left stored away here. My room has been crowded all day with students. Health improving slowly. Weather very beautiful.

Aug. 31st.

There has been very little done in the way of study, as we had only two lessons assigned and these were short. The faculty have been employed in the examination of new students.

Sept. 1st.

Owing to the confusion still existing in the arrangements of the recitations of each class, we merely went through the motions today in the way of recitation. Paid $20 to Mrs. Hughes toward my board. Weather pleasant and health improving.

Sept. 2nd.

Our recitations went on today with but little confusion and were very well attended generally. It rained very hard this afternoon, so that the air is much cooler. I have felt badly all day, having the headache, and a disease not uncommon among students, denominated, in general, the "Blues."

Sept. 3rd.

Hall met; nothing done except election of officers. Weather pleasant. Health improving. Retire to bed at 12.

Sept. 4th.

It was so late before I got up that I came near losing my breakfast. Applied to Dr. Anderson this morning for permission to study the German language instead of Calculus, which I obtained, provided that during the Junior year I will not call myself regular. Went out in the country this afternoon with Dr. Huston in his carriage, to his farm, where we got plenty of the finest kind of apples. Got back in time for supper, quite tired; got to bed at 10.

Sept. 5th. Sabbath.

On account of not hearing, or rather of mistaking, the Chapel bell this morning, I was not present at the regular morning service and of course was absent from Bible class also. Attended preaching in the Methodist Church at 11, and in the afternoon stayed in my room. Go to bed at 10.

Sept. 6th.
I have three recitations to make tomorrow between the hours of 8 and
11, only one of which is prepared. Retire to bed at 11, hoping to be up
early. Health improving.

Sept. 7th & 8th.
Got through with my recitations much better than I had anticipated.
Our class had a lecture by Prof. Stoddard on the "Laws of Motion."
This took the place of a recitation. Health about the same. Weather
damp and cool. Wrote to my friend, R. P. Adams, of Lexington, Geor-
gia.

Sept. 9th. & 10th.
I have been very busily occupied these two days, as in addition to my
regular recitations, I have prepared a declamation for halls, which
however I did not deliver, as I happened to have business which called
me out at the time my name was called. A new Constitution had its
first reading this afternoon and was laid on the table. Our "sessional
speeches" were delivered this evening by the following gentlemen: L.
M. Bonham, Jos. McNutt, W. S. McNair, and J. W. Steel. Mr. Hutcheson, on motion, was excused, as he said, owing to circumstances over
which he had no control, he was unprepared. After choosing a question for debate we adjourned. Health same. Retire to bed at 1 o'clock.

Sept. 11th & 12th.
After our regular Chapel exercise this morning, I prepared my Greek
lesson for Monday. In the afternoon it rained very hard, so that I could
not be out, so I occupied myself in miscellaneous reading and talking.
Being much troubled with the toothache, I do not get to bed until after midnight. Sent to Cincinnati and got a German Testament. [12th.]
Sabbath. I attended Bible class in college under Prof. Stoddard at 8
a.m. Attend preaching in the New School Presbyterian Church at 11,
and again at 7 p.m. Read one volume of Harriet B. Stowe's *Uncle
Tom's Cabin*[28] and one chapter in my German Testament. Feeling
quite sleepy, I retire to bed at 9.

Sept. 13th & 14th.
The weather has been very damp and so cool that we have been obliged to keep a fire all the time, and in consequence of this I have not felt so well as usual, have had the toothache, headache, and in fact a general assortment of the latest and most fashionable aches.

Sept. 15th & 16th.
The weather still cool, though not so wet. Feel weak, and the want of exercise. I have stuck closely to my books, but it seemed as though "the spirit was willing but the flesh was weak." Write a short letter to cousin A. H. Sharp.

Sept. 17.
Weather quite pleasant. Health much better. Take considerable exercise in sawing wood. Hall met this afternoon. Mr. Brooks of Tennessee read a first-rate essay of about a half hour's length. Adjourned to meet next Friday on account of preaching this evening.

Sept. 18th & 19th.
Prepare my Greek lesson for Monday, first thing after Chapel exercises were over. In the afternoon, answer a letter received from brother Ira by today's mail. Write a letter to Cousin Annie Sharp. [19th] Sabbath. Attend church at 11 and hear a good sermon delivered by the Rev. Mr. Worrell, the Old School Presbyterian minister of this place. During the afternoon read German Testament. Health about the same. Retire to bed at 10:30 o'clock.

Sept. 20th & 21st.
I have passed these two days quite pleasantly, as I have felt better than usual, on account of the pleasant weather. I have studied with much more satisfaction to myself. Sat up last night till after midnight to write a letter to Stewart Slavens. Commenced a letter tonight to Mrs. Buell, but I feel so sleepy, I will leave it off for some other time.

Sept. 22nd. & 23rd.
Our class have gotten through these two days without much study, as we had lectures and experiments by Prof. Stoddard on Mechanics, in-

stead of recitations. I was informed this evening by Theo McLean of
my election to membership in the Phi Delta Theta Society, which was
accepted. 23rd. Initiated this evening at 10 o'clock in the order of the
Phi Delta Theta Society, B chapter, and by request was transferred to
the A Chapter.[29]

Sept. 24th.
Bought one-half cord of wood, and also paid my sessional tax. Society
met, passed a new constitution; much disorder and hard feeling. I was
fined for disorder, but appealed and Society decided in my favor.

Sept. 25th.
I did not get to bed last night until about one o'clock, in consequence
of which did not get up this morning till after breakfast, but Mrs.
Hughes prepared me some. Chapel exercises this morning continued
until nearly 10 o'clock. We had a very witty speech by William Tor-
rents, "on college boys hooking chickens." After he was through and
the burst of laughter had subsided, the President remarked that everyone, as a general thing, took a subject with which they were well acquainted, and which was suited to their talents and inclinations; this
caused a great laugh. After Chapel I studied until dinner time, after
which I sawed wood till night. Read the greater part of the last copy of
the *Knickerbocker* [magazine] sent to me by Pa. Get out my clean
clothes and retire to bed at 10:30 o'clock.

Sept. 26th. Sabbath.
Weather cool. Feel very tired and sore from sawing wood. Stay in my
room all day.

Sept. 27th & 28th.
I have been in a great hurry all day, as my extra recitation in German
came off today. Phi Delta Theta Society met at 1 p.m. and initiated
Mr. Rafter from Tennessee, who expects to leave for Texas tomorrow.
A copy of the Constitution, etc., was presented to him, with the power
to establish a chapter of said Society at the College to which he is go-
ing.[30] I am very sorry to see one of my Tennessee friends leave.
Health very good. 28th. Rafter left. Weather cool. Received a visit in

my room this evening from Mr. McLean, one of my particular friends. Feel physically well, but very sad and low spirited. Go to bed at 11:30.

Sept. 29th & 30th.
Got up at 4:30; built a fire, walked a mile with Mr. Hussey, who rooms near me, and came back so as to be ready for breakfast. I have felt uncommonly well today. Retire at 10:30. I will sleep on the floor by the fire as my roommate is unwell. 30th. A great many of the students went to Hamilton today to the State Fair, and there was also a balloon ascension there. We saw the balloon from the college.

Oct. 1st and & 2nd.
Hall met at the usual hours. In the afternoon, the regular business was dispensed with for the election of the Winter exhibition speakers, and consequently I did not get the opportunity of reading my essay, the preparation of which had cost so much trouble. In the evening session we had a very pleasant debate. Question, "Should Parents and guardians be required by law to educate their children?" Decision in favor of the Negative. 2nd. Feel quite unwell today and have done very little studying. Take a Blue Pill tonight.

Oct. 3rd. Sabbath.
Attend Chapel and Bible class, after which I scarcely left my room. Medicine operated well, and I feel much better tonight.

Oct. 4th & 5th.
I have made poorer recitations today than I have ever done since I came to Miami University. Feel **very** unwell. I begin to feel stupid again and think I will take more medicine if there is not a change for the better soon. Bought one and a half cords of wood and sawed part of it.

Oct. 6th & 7th.
I have been studying well these two days and have made first-rate recitations. Received a copy of an address delivered before the Theological students of the Seminary at Cincinnati by Prof. J. C. Moffatt. I judge my friend David Swing[31] sent it, who is a student at that place.

Received a letter from my friend R. P. Adams of Lexington, Georgia. I feel a little better than I did a few days since, as I have dieted myself.

Oct. 8th & 9th.
Hall met. Had quite a pleasant debate this evening. Question, "Should the Maine Liquor Law be established in Ohio?"[32] 9th. Studied until dinner time. Went to Post Office after dinner and was disappointed, for I was almost certain of getting a letter from home. Sawed wood till five o'clock. Too tired to study tonight; retire to bed at 10 o'clock. Health tolerably good.

Oct. 10th. Sabbath.
Feel quite tired from my yesterday's work. Read part of German Testament. Weather clear and cool.

Oct. 11th & 12th.
John B. Welles, U.S. Senator from California, spoke in town this afternoon. I did not attend, though I heard that there was much excitement, and a difficulty arose between the students and town. Smiley, a student, threw something in the crowd; it was resented by someone; this brought all the students to Smiley's assistance, but as the students were greatly surpassed in numbers, they permitted it to cease. 12th. The election of Congressmen and some other civil officers came off today. Temperance Society met tonight, after which the students determined to have satisfaction for yesterday's work, and marched on the town with the implements of war afforded by mother earth, but not a town boy was to be found out of his room. Received a letter from Miss J. E. Miller which I answered today. I have studied well, sawed wood for exercise, and feel quite well. Weather has been quite cool, though clear and healthy. I will now lie down on the floor by my stove at 12 o'clock. Hoping to be up at 4.

Oct. 13th & 14th.
Recitations have been very good; better rather than usual. Weather cool, clear, and healthy. The hostility between the town and college boys still exists; though there is not so much excitement, yet no one

goes to town without a weapon of some kind. Health has been good, except the toothache, occasionally.

Oct. 15th & 16th.
Hall met; my performance was declamation, which I got through with, with rather more self-possession than usual. All the performances were quite interesting, and some very witty, especially Owens and Steel. Sawed and carried up considerable wood. Saturday, 16th. Read over German and Greek lessons, which took about half the time. The other part of the day has been spent in "loafing." Retire to bed at 10. I was very much disappointed, as I fully expected a letter from home today.

Oct. 17th.
Feel worse today than I have since I have come to Oxford. Take a large Blue Pill. Retire to bed at 10.

Oct. 18th & 19th.
My medicine operated during the forenoon, which made me quite sick. I missed only one recitation. During the afternoon I had a very severe toothache; went to Dr. Huston to get it extracted, which he declined doing, as he said it would require a good deal of skill and advised me to go to a Dentist. It is easier tonight, but I intend having something done with it if it pains me much more. 19th. Got up at 4 as usual and brought up what lessons were behind. Feel badly today. Go to bed at 10.

Oct. 20th & 21st.
Feel better today and have done a good day's work. 21st. Toothache again, worse than it had ever been; went to the Dentist and got it extracted; it was very hard to pull. On this account I am behind with my lessons. Torchlight procession and political speaking in town tonight; a jollification among the Whigs over Mr. Campbell's election. I did not attend. Feel well tonight except a pain in my breast. Retire at 11.

Oct. 22nd & 23rd.
Society met. Election of officers. I was elected Recording Secretary,

after which there were some resolutions offered, which were the preparatory steps for expelling Mr. E. E. Hutcheson from the Society for signing Messrs. Ross and Lane's diplomas and also for depriving Ross and Lane from being honorary members. After much quarreling, a motion for the indefinite postponement was carried; but notice was given that it would be brought up at the next meeting of the Society, which I think according to Cushing's Manual can't be done, and this is our standard. 23rd. Prepare recitations for Monday. During the afternoon read and loaf. The news came of Daniel Webster's death. Feel quite well, but very "blue" on account of not getting a letter from home. Commenced to write, but concluded that it would not be a good policy if I wished to hear from there.

Oct. 24th. Sabbath.
Attended Church twice, once to hear Mr. Chalfant and once to hear Mr. Tenny. Weather cool. Health good. Retire at 9:30 o'clock.

Oct. 25th & 26th.
I have gotten along today much better than I usually do on Mondays, my recitations having been much better prepared for on Saturday. Received a letter from brother Ira today, which afforded less satisfaction than any letter I ever received from him; there was very little of it, anyway. Two students came near being burned to death a few minutes since, their can of Phosgene Gas having been set on fire through their own carelessness.

Oct. 26th.
Dr. Anderson has gone to New Albany. Prof. Stoddard hears our class in his place in Natural Theology. The students act as though they think they are free when he is away. Mend my pants and sew some buttons on my shirts tonight. As I have adopted the rule of getting up at 4, I must go to bed at 10 or thereabouts.

Oct. 27th & 28th.
I have been quite busy today, more so than usual; do not get to bed till 12. 28th. Got up at 3:30, or rather lit my lamp at that time, for I did not go to bed, only laid down on the floor and took a nap. Answer Ira's letter.

Oct. 29th & 30th.
Hall met this afternoon; the regular business was postponed and Mr.
Helm introduced the resolutions again which were indefinitely postponed on last Friday. According to parliamentary law, they could not
be brought up; but the opposition finding that they had the majority,
voted it parliamentary and adopted the resolutions with some amend-
ments so as not to expel Hutcheson. An attempt will be made next
meeting to do away with them. I was inducted secretary, and as we had
a long meeting and the yeas and nays were called on every motion, I
found it a very difficult task to fill my office. Do not get to bed until 3
a.m. Oct. 30th. Arranged the minutes of the Society, got Greek lessons
for Monday, and read part of a *Knickerbocker* which came today. Received a letter from Miss Miller, also one from G. W. Ralston at
Lebanon College. Animal show in town this evening; did not attend.
Answered Miss Miller's letter, also Ralston's. Weather cool. Health
good. Retire to bed at 10 o'clock.

Oct. 31st.
This day has been cool and disagreeable; stayed in my room nearly all
the time and read.

Nov. 1st & 2nd.
Got up this morning at about 3 o'clock and prepared my Natural Philosophy lesson before breakfast. Hruby, Professor of German and
French, assigned lessons today to his respective classes. Weather cool.
Retire at 11 o'clock. I have not been to bed for two or three weeks. I
sleep on the carpet with my feet to the fire, which I keep up all night.
2nd. Up at 4. As I have had comparatively little to do today, I have
read the greater part of my last *Knickerbocker*. Health moderately
good. Lie down at 10. This was the day in which the Presidential election was held.[33]

Nov. 3rd & 4th.
Got up each morning at 4. Studied well. Commenced recitations to
Prof. Hruby in German. Weather has been wet and disagreeable. Received letters, one from J. F. Bailey, one from Miss Lizzie Sharp, one
from J. L. Cannon, and one from Robert Morrison. Loaned my *Knick-*

erbockers to Prof. Bishop, who is my favorite among the faculty. Had a controversy with Mr. Hussey on the parsing of a Latin sentence. Prof. Bishop decided in my favor.

Nov. 5th & 6th.
Hall met this afternoon at the usual hour. Regular business was dispensed with. The minutes of last meeting, which had reference to the resolutions offered, were expunged by a small majority. Evening session. Hutcheson indicted and arraigned by the Censor, to answer to the charge of signing his name as President to the diplomas of Messrs. Lewis Ross and Isaac Lane. Found guilty. Penalty balloted for, which resulted as follows: Reprimand one. Suspension seven. Expulsion eight. Fine 24. So he was fined one dollar. The prosecutors were J. C. Ross, Censor, and H. T. Helm. Defendants were E. E. Hutcheson and Alexander Telford. It kept me quite busy to keep the minutes, as the yeas and nays were called a good many times. 6th. Lend Prof. Bishop my *Knickerbocker* for **this** month. Have a good deal of company in my room. Study some and write one letter. Retire to bed at 11.

Nov. 7th. Sabbath.
Read German Testament until dinner. After dinner, slept till nearly night, as the weather was so cold that there was no inducement to be out of my room and I had lost a good deal of sleep.

Nov. 8th & 9th.
Copied for Mr. Hutcheson the long minutes of Miami Union Society taken two weeks since. Retire at 12. Nov. 9th. Had experiments in Prof. Stoddard's department, instead of a recitation, which made our recitations easier today than usual. Attended a debate of the College Temperance Society this evening. Speakers on the affirmative, Messrs. Hutcheson and Ustic; on the negative, Messrs. Atherton and Morgan. The question was, "Should the Maine Liquor Law be adopted in Ohio?" Hutcheson came to my room about 9 p.m. to bid me farewell; he is to leave this place for Columbus in the morning, as he is to be Reporter for the state in the Legislature. Weather cold. Retire to bed at 10 o'clock.

Nov. 10th & 11th.
Did not wake this morning until nearly 6, on which account my recitations have not been so good as usual. Board of Trustees met today, elected Mr. T. Wylie Professor of Mathematics, and changed the
course of study by making Greek optional, by inserting in its stead a
full four years' course of both French and German.[34] 11th. Attend a
meeting of the Phi Delta Theta Society in John Anderson's room.

Nov. 12th & 13th.
Met in Chapel this morning at the usual hour. President Anderson announced the death of Professor Matthews, who had been sick in
Cincinnati for some time. Regular college duties suspended for today.
The students remained in Chapel after prayers and passed some resolutions expressing their sorrow for the loss of such a friend to the University and such an accomplished scholar as professor. Hall met this
afternoon, but, as a tribute of respect to Prof. Matthews, deceased, adjourned to meet next Friday at the usual hour. Copied the minutes of
last meeting of the Society. Prepared a Greek lesson for Monday and
retired to bed at 11 o'clock. 13th. After chapel exercises, I sawed wood
until dinner time, and after dinner carried up the wood which I had
sawed. When I got through, I was too tired to study, so as I received a
letter from Brother Ira today, I answered it. Go to bed at 10.

Nov. 14th.
Got up at 6 o'clock. Stayed in my room all day, as the weather has been
very cold, and read 10 chapters in the German Testament. Snowed
enough to cover the ground. Health good.

Nov. 15th & 16th.
Snowed constantly nearly all day. Received a letter from J. W. Lindly.
Feel quite happy as my health is good, and although the weather is
cold and disagreeable, yet I have a close room, a nice little stove, and
plenty of wood sawed to burn in it. 16th. Snow partly melted off. Show
in town tonight. I did not attend. As Dr. Anderson was unwell today,
we had quite an easy time, as we had one recitation less.

Nov. 17th & 18th.
I have been very busy today, as in addition to my three regular recita-

tions, I have transcribed the By-Laws of the Miami Union Literary Society. Retire to bed at 11 o'clock. 18th. Got up at 5 o'clock. Besides my regular duties, I have answered a letter from my friend J. W. Lindly. Received a *Knickerbocker* from home. Snowed nearly all day, but the ground was too warm for it to remain long in the form of snow. Missed one of my recitations today on account of mistaking the time. Take 15 minutes exercise on the campus at football. Fight between Wm. Lowe and J. Matson.

Nov. 19th & 20th.
Society met. All the duties were performed regularly and all hostilities seem to have been forgotten. In the evening session, we had quite an interesting debate on the question, "Should theatres and theatrical compositions be discarded?" Found no difficulty in taking the minutes. Wm. Owens made his usual amount of wit on a declamation. 20th. Chapel performances were more interesting this morning than usual. Mr. Brooks of Tennessee made a long and exciting speech in fa· vor of slavery. Much cheering and the chapel was crowded. Sawed wood. Very tired tonight. Go to bed early.

Nov. 21st.
This day has been quite cold and dreary. Stayed close to my fire and books all day. Feel quite unwell from a bad cold, which seems to affect my lungs principally. Drink some of the brandy with which my father provided me before leaving home and retire to bed early.

Nov. 22nd & 23rd.
Commenced review in Dr. Anderson's department today, 40 pages for the first lesson, only able to read over a lesson once. Gave Charles Brown, my friend who is now sick, some brandy, as he is my patient.

Nov. 24th & 25th.
Weather damp and quite uncomfortable. Missed German recitation by mistaking the time. 25th. Thanksgiving day. College duties suspended. Rev. Tenny delivered an eulogy on Daniel Webster about three hours in length. Feel quite unwell this evening from having eaten too much dinner, as Mrs. Hughes gave us something better than usual and it was late coming. Did not go to supper.

Nov. 26th & 27th.
I was well prepared for recitations today, but most of the class gave in their usual excuse, viz., sick. Hall met this evening; quite an interesting time. Got out tonight at 10 o'clock. 27th. Saturday, Drew off the minutes of the Miami Union Literary Society, and afterwards prepared Monday's lessons. Weather too cold to saw any wood and take exercise of any kind. Wrote a letter in answer to one received from Miss J. E. Miller by today's mail.

Nov. 28th. Sabbath.
Waked this morning with so bad a cold that I found it almost impossible to speak loud enough to be heard across the room. My breast also pains me. Took a walk of about two miles and when I got back I was very much exhausted. Have the "blues" the worst kind.

Nov. 29th & 30th.
Up at 5 o'clock so as to be thoroughly prepared for recitations. Cold no better; coughed a good deal this evening. 30th. Cold has begun to get better, though my cough is worse. Received a letter from my former teacher, Wm. Buell, D.D. Society met this afternoon to elect someone to fill the place of Mr. McNutt on the coming exhibition, as he on account of ill health has declined. Mr. Helm of Indiana was elected, on which account Mr. Steele declined also, as he was anxious that Mr. McNair should be elected.

Dec. 1st & 2nd.
I have done but little at study on account of poor health. Cold no better, rather worse. I have coughed more today than I have done any day yet. Answered Rev. W. T. Buell's letter.

Dec. 3rd.
Society met. Good order and creditable performance. No meeting during evening as there is church in town and also a panorama. Wrote the minutes of last meeting, after which I had intended to have studied, but James Ireland came in my room and as usual we got into a discussion, so that it is now 11 o'clock.

Dec. 4th & 5th. Saturday.

After having prepared Monday's lessons, I sawed wood as long as I could stand it. Wrote a long letter tonight to Lafayette Cannon. 5th. Feel quite unwell. Cold is some better; coughed much this evening. Walked about two miles. Retire to bed early.

Dec. 6th & 7th.

Dr. Anderson absent and the students "cut up" ridiculously in chapel this morning. Weather disagreeable. Health some better. Received a letter from Alfred H. Sharp chiding me very much for not having written to him in more than two months. This I answered. Retire to bed at 10.

Dec. 8th & 9th.

On account of Prof. Stoddard's giving us lectures and experiments in Electricity, our class are now having a remarkably easy time of it. My spare moments have been taken up in reading German. Phi Delta Theta held a meeting tonight in John Anderson's room; made preparations for our regular annual festival. Committee of arrangements: J. A. Anderson, E. Shields, and P. C. Conklin. After the meeting was over, we retired to Clute's and had some pies and cider; this it fell to my lot to pay for. On the whole we had a first rate time of it. Go to bed at 11.

Dec. 10th & 11th.

Hall met. Irregular business attended to, and as usual on such occasions very much disorder. Election of speakers for the beginning of next session was attended to. Speakers elected were Cortelyou, Killen, Colmery, Williams, and T. C. Hibbett. I had expected to have some time for recreation this vacation, but to see the A's carry the day touched my heartstrings, so by the earnest solicitations of the Phis I accepted, though I fear that I'll make a poor orator. 11th. This day has been spent in writing a composition for the Phi Delta Theta Society, as we expect to have another meeting before our feast, at which all will be expected to perform. I have also commenced reading Washington Irving's biography of Oliver Goldsmith. This, not unlike all Irving's writings, is very attractive and interesting. Cough no better.

Dec. 12th. Sabbath.
I have been quite unwell today, though my cough, I fancy, is getting better. Weather so very cold that I did not take any exercise as I had intended. Read Irving's Goldsmith half through. Retire to bed at 10. Dr. Anderson preached in chapel this afternoon.

Dec. 13th & 14th.
Our lessons have been for the most part general reviews; for instance, in Dr. Anderson's department we had the whole of Mental Philosophy, in Prof. Stoddard's, the whole of Natural Philosophy that we have gone over this session, etc. Spent what spare time I had taking notes on my studies for examinations, some of which I have lost and consequently will have my work to do over again. The students, especially those whom Dr. Anderson sometimes refers to as will probably graduate soon, have been in all kinds of mischief, especially "hooking" Chambers's chickens and turkeys, playing at cards, etc. Received a letter from Mother, but will not answer it until after examinations.

Dec. 15th & 16th.
I have occupied myself today in finishing the life of Dr. Goldsmith, as after recitations were over we had nothing of college duties to attend to, for this is the last day for recitations this session. Someone hooked part of our wood which was sawed; found out it was Joe Fullerton, whom I have been furnishing in wood all winter, as he has been looking for a load of his own for the last two months. He is not satisfied with sawing wood from any pile, but must have some that's already sawed.

Dec. 17th & 18th.
Finished Irving's *Bracebridge Hall,* though it took me till about midnight. There was a "chicken frolic" in the room adjoining me tonight, I think. Chambers must have lost a dozen [to judge] from the squalling, for I think part of the crowd were tight, as they let them loose in the room. 18th. Examined in Mental Philosophy and have finished some miscellaneous reading on hand. Retire to bed at 12.

Dec. 19th.
Read the whole of the Greek over that we have reviewed this session,

and copied the minutes of the Society. Answered the letter which I received from home a few days since. As I have of late lost a good deal of sleep, retire to bed at 9.

Dec. 20th.
Examined in Natural Philosophy, and Greek. Attend an exhibition of the Erodelphian Society this evening. Speakers: Homes, Ustic, Mc-Clung, and Galbreath, after which we adjourned to Clute's Saloon, where we found the finest supper that I ever sat to prepared for us. After initiating Ransford Smith, we ate supper; our annual festival, 20 present including old members. Retire to bed at 1 o'clock a.m.

Dec. 21st.
Examined in Greek and Natural Theology. Examinations closed today, and as far as I have learned, all passed very creditably. At least the committee of examiners were highly flattered at our progress. The exhibition of the Miami Union Literary Society was held this evening in the Old School Presbyterian Church. Speakers were Hibbern, Morgan, Helm, Steele, Atherton, and James H. Brooks of Tennessee. Mr. Brooks became very much excited and spoke most of the time extemporaneously; his speech left an impression on all present. His subject was "the true work." Steele's was very witty: subject, "woman's rights." I have been quite unwell today, from having eaten too much at the Phi supper last night.

Dec. 22nd.
My roommate left me today, to spend his vacation at home. Nearly all the students left this morning. Spent the day in cleaning up my room, so as to be ready to go at my speech on tomorrow. Felt very lonely; wrote to Miss Miller. Paid my room rent for this and the next session. Drew four dollars from Prof. Bishop to bear my expenses this vacation.

Dec. 23rd & 24th.
Being all alone today, and feeling somewhat at a loss to know what to do at first, as I have a great many things laid off to attend to during this vacation, I at last concluded that my speech had better be attended to first, so as to get it off my mind, so I went right at it and finished it tonight at 9 o'clock. Borrowed Morrison's clock during this vacation, so

as to cause Mrs. Hughes no trouble by being too late at meal time.
24th. Read 200 pages in *Crayon Miscellany* by Irving. As this is Christmas Eve, I can hear some sport going on in town, in the line of
creating a noise; no one has discovered my solitary light in this long
building as yet, i.e., they have not indicated such a thing by their presence.

Dec. 25th.
This I presume was Christmas Day. Yes, it was, if I mistake not. Oh
yes, I recollect now, I saw some little boys enjoying themselves with
shooting crackers at the market house as I went to the post office
at noon. There are only three of our boarders remaining, but Mrs.
Hughes gave us as usual a good dinner, which we took at 2 o'clock, and
went without supper. I was bored all the forenoon by visitors, so I read
none. Since dinner, I have read the *Crayon Miscellany* through.

Dec. 26th & 27th.
The weather has been very disagreeable; spent the day in miscellane-
ous reading. Go to bed at 12. 27th. Read 400 pages in Irving's *Sketch
Book*. Got wet in coming from supper tonight, and I fear I'll have an-
other cold. Received a letter from J. L. Cannon, as usual very witty.
Retire to bed at 12 o'clock.

Dec. 28th & 29th.
Finish Irving's *Sketch Book*, which is all the reading that I have done
today. Weather very cold. Sawed some wood late this afternoon. 29th.
Read a short sketch of the life of Thomas Paine, and have determined
to write a speech on him. Retire to bed at 10 o'clock.

Dec. 30th & 31st.
Weather has been quite cold, and as I have had to burn a great deal of
wood, so much of my time has been taken up in sawing, which is an art
I find very difficult to learn. Read part of the life of Mary, Queen of
Scots, by Abbott. 31st. Finished the life of Mary, Queen of Scots,
which I am free to say is the most affecting thing I have ever read. Attempted to read some of Carlyle's writing, but I abhor his style so
much I think of leaving it off.[35] There is a great deal of excitement in
town tonight among the small "fry," as this is New Year's Eve.

Elliott Hall today still looks much as it did in T. C. Hibbett's time, when it was known simply as North Dorm. But in earlier days, every room had to be furnished by the students who lived in it, and every fireplace had to be stoked with wood they chopped themselves, for their only source of heat.

1853

Jan. 1st & 2nd.

The year ushered in with no excitement for me, except the hope of getting a letter, as I am becoming somewhat lonesome. This however I failed at, to my dissatisfaction. I have done very little today in anything. Visited my friend Brooks this evening and spent several hours very pleasantly. Retire at 12 o'clock. 2nd. Spent the day in lounging about. Read some in my German Testament. Had "Red" Morrison to visit me this evening and sit several hours. This was a "little bore."

Jan. 3rd & 4th.

These two days have been employed in writing my speech for the Society. My subject is "Individual Fame, Thomas Paine." My views of this individual, I know, are not orthodox; nevertheless, I live in a free country, and the object of my life is not to please the world by going against my conscience to advocate what the majority believe. I am not an aspirant to fame and therefore have nothing to lose on that score.

Jan. 5th & 6th.

I have spent these two days in cleaning my room. Took up my carpet, and got new straw to put under it. Shaking an old carpet is the dirtiest work connected with the duties of my room. Charles Brown, Jonathan Stewart, and myself made some egg nog tonight and had a little spree. No one got tight and everything went off jovially. Go to bed at 10 o'clock.

Jan. 7th & 8th.

Vacation is getting to be a "bore." Wrote to J. L. Cannon, J. C. Ireland, Miss Lizzie Sharp. Read about 250 pages in Irving's *Knickerbocker's History of New York*. After shaving and getting out some clean clothes, go to bed at 10 o'clock.

Jan. 9th. Sabbath.

Went to Associated Reformed Church this forenoon and heard Dr. Claybaugh. Read German Testament this afternoon, and attended church this evening and heard Mr. Dill. Feel very lonely tonight, as everyone who remained during vacation are now gone out to the country.

Jan. 10th & 11th.

As Wilson, who was teaching near our house in Tennessee, has been staying with me, I have done but little these two days. Committed most of my speech, which I find to be more difficult than it was to write it at first.[36] After writing a letter to J. W. Lindley, retire to bed.

Jan. 12th & 13th.

Finished reading Irving's *Knickerbocker's History of New York,* which scared off an attack of his Satanic Majesty in the shape of the "blues." Put in about a half dozen panes of glass and washed my windows off, so that I'm ready for the session to begin, with the exception of some plastering and blacking my stove. Looked in vain for a letter from home, and have been tempted to write to them by way of rousing them up with the sad news that I am very sick, but this would not be right. Go to bed at 12.

Jan. 14th & 15th.

Weather not very cold. Wrote part of an essay for hall, read some of the life of Mary, Queen of England, by Lingard, and painted my writing desk. Resolved to begin the study of French, but I will have to overtake a class which began last session. Very few students have as yet come in. I have not been very well since my last record; have had an uneasiness in my breast, occasioned by stooping over the table in writing. Retire to bed at 11 o'clock.

Jan. 16th.

The weather has been clear but quite cold. Health not very good; spent the day in reading an account of the religious persecutions under Queen Mary of England. Go to bed at 10.

Jan. 17th & 18th.

College commenced today; only about 50 present at chapel, though a good many more came on the 12 o'clock stages. 18th. About 100 at chapel; we meet the professors at their respective recitation rooms and had lessons assigned. Weather very cold; on the night stages there came a jolly set of students, all pretty tight. Such joy when all meet! Even those who were formerly enemies shake hands.

Jan. 19th & 20th.
Roommate came back today in fine health and spirits. Looked in vain for a letter from home. Weather clear, but so cold that the ground remained frozen. Our recitations have gone on regularly, but very little has been done. Our new Professor, Theophilus S. Wylie, has entered on his duties. My health has been very good.

Jan. 21st & 22nd.
Society met, but no business was transacted. I succeeded in getting Wm. McNair elected President. He, though a Delta, [probably Delta Kappa Epsilon, or "Deke" — see Note 21 for further explanation] has always been very friendly to the Phis. I did not permit my name to be run for any office, though much urged. No meeting in the evening. Attend the Oxford Lyceum and heard some good speeches on capital punishment from Professor Elliott, Reverend Worrell and others. 22nd. Had a recitation in German at 9 a.m., after which I prepared Monday's recitations, which kept me very busy, as I had other business to attend to as secretary of the Society. The ground is now covered with snow, and there is a prospect of having a good sleighing time.

Jan. 23rd.
After Bible class, I occupied myself with miscellaneous reading. Attend preaching in chapel. Sleighs beginning to run. Retire to bed at 10 o'clock.

Jan. 24th & 25th.
Weather has been extremely cold, and on this account I have not been out of my room, except to get my meals. My time has been well employed, as I have been trying to overtake the Senior Class in French. Plead to get off from Greek Prose Composition, but could not come it, so I have to be content with four recitations per diem. My reading of the History of England, I fear, will fall through. No letter from home yet. Room has been infested with company, rather more than I like, but there is no remedy unless I insult them.

Jan. 26th & 27th.
Weather still very cold. Recitations all went off better than I could
have expected, except one to Prof. Stoddard, when the whole class
failed, and we have to get the lesson over again. This never happened
before since I've been in college. Received a letter today from my
mother and answered it this evening. Attend Phi meeting tonight and
was elected Secretary.

Jan. 28th & 29th.
Society met and the regular business was gone through with by way of
making a beginning. Sessional speeches came off tonight. Hall crowded with girls. I got through much better than I had expected, but became too much excited to deliver my speech with much ease. 29th. I
have been very unwell today, occasioned by the excitement I went
through with last night. Have done nothing except to square up my
business as Secretary of the Society and recite in German.

Jan. 30th. Sabbath.
As I was very unwell I did not go to church, but stayed in my room all
day after Bible class, until about 4 o'clock, when I took a walk and felt
better afterwards.

Jan. 31st & Feb. 1st.
These two days, to use a common expression, have been a bore. Although my recitations have all been attended to, yet I have not felt like
study. Took a long walk this afternoon. Weather quite pleasant.

Feb. 2nd & 3rd.
My birthday. Weather damp and disagreeable. Feel no better. I and
Doctor Anderson got at loggerheads on Evidences of Christianity.
Both got angry.

Feb. 4th & 5th.
Hall met. During the afternoon we had an excellent performance in
the way of essays and declamations. In the evening we had what is
called a "stag debate." Sat. 5th. Prepared Monday's lessons and read
100 pages in the life of Henry VIII of England. Weather very cold.

Feb. 6th. Sabbath.
Did not go to Bible class this morning as Prof. Stoddard never calls any roll; but I have since heard that the roll was called **this** morning, and as I have no excuse I can't tell how to get out of it. Heard Dr. Anderson in chapel this afternoon. It moderated some last night, and the snow is now about 8 inches in depth. Retire to bed at 10.

Feb. 7th & 8th.
Nothing of uncommon importance to record. The weather has been extremely cold, though the sun has shone out all day, and there is no sign of the snow melting. Much sleighing going on. Finished Henry VIII.

Feb. 9th & 10th.
Weather still very uncomfortable. Recitations have not been very good, on account of not having time to prepare all sufficiently well, as I have two extra studies. Health not very good. Attended Phi meeting, and we squared off our bill with Clute. As but few were present, we adjourned "without a meeting" until this night week. Go to bed at 12.

Feb. 11th & 12th.
The weather has so much moderated that the snow has begun to melt. Had quite an interesting time at Hall this evening. Question for discussion, "Should the dead languages receive the attention in our colleges which they now do?" After making preparation for Monday, I wrote a letter to my friend Oliver P. Long at Farmer's College.

Feb. 13th.
The weather has been very stormy. Prof. Stoddard delivered us quite an interesting lecture in Bible class this morning on the 3rd Chapter of Daniel. Spent the day in reading. Health only moderately good. Retire to bed at 10 o'clock.

Feb. 14th & 15th.
St. Valentine's Day. Great sport going in the way of letters. Received one Valentine, also received a letter from home and one from Miss J. E. Miller at Nashville. Answered both. Weather very disagreeable.

Wrote an essay for Hall. Have been very busy indeed. Health by no means good. Feel the want of exercise very much.

Feb. 16th & 17th.
I have been very busy indeed these two days, have answered several long letters, and besides been pretty well prepared on my recitations. Weather disagreeable. Snow melting off. Health only moderately good.

Feb. 18th & 19th.
Hall met; read a composition which was severely criticized. We had quite an interesting time during the afternoon, though but few were out. Question for discussion, "Has a state a right to nullify an act of Congress?" 19th. First news this morning was of the death of one of our students; A. Thrall died this morning about 2 o'clock. He first had the measles, but had gotten better and took cold. Preparations are being made for his interment, as all his friends are absent. Much excitement.

Feb. 20th.
Mr. Thrall's funeral took place today in chapel, by Dr. Anderson. The chapel was crowded, and a good many had to stay out. The Erodelphian Society, to which Mr. Thrall belonged, furnished him with a $25 metal coffin, which was sealed up and deposited in their library until we shall get some word from his mother. The corpse will be taken to her if she prefers.

Feb. 21st & 22nd.
The weather has been remarkably pleasant, except some rain this afternoon. I have finished the eighth volume of Lingard's England, and will now go back to the first, so as to bring it all up regularly. Prayer meetings are being held every evening, with a view of getting up a revival.

Feb. 23rd & 24th.
As Mr. Thrall's mother arrived at Oxford last evening and determined to take his body home for interment, we met as a college at 1 o'clock

p.m. today, and, marching double file with the faculty in front, accompanied the corpse to the edge of town. 24th. As today has been appointed for prayer for colleges, we have had no recitations, but the day has been spent in prayer by most of the students. Commenced writing a speech on "Poverty and its connections with Greatness," but did but little at it.

Feb. 25th & 26th.

Hall met. Question for discussion this evening, "Has the world been influenced more by physical than moral causes?" I was leader of the division on the Affirmative, but had the question decided in favor of Ran. Smith, the leader of the opposition. 26th. Temperance Society met tonight; question debated, "Should the production of native wine be discouraged?" McNutt made a speech which did honor to the Union Hall.

Feb. 27th. Sabbath.

Attended church in the forenoon and heard a sermon by Mr. Worrell on the subject of the obligation of Christians to become ministers in preference to any other profession. As it rained very hard, I did not go out this evening, but read my German Testament, which I can now read almost as easily as English. Health moderately good. Retire to bed early, as I did not sleep much last night.

Feb. 28th & March 1st.

As Prof. Elliott has been unwell, and our lessons were consequently not so numerous, I have had time to read, but have been extensively bored by my friends. Sent to Cincinnati by Morrison for some French books. Weather rainy, and disagreeable.

March 2nd & 3rd.

Weather cold. Preaching will be held in all the churches, every day during this week, as next Sabbath sacrament will be administered. The revival thus far has failed, except in the Methodist Church. Health not good. Attend Phi meeting tonight in Anderson's room. Not much done on account of there being but few present.

March 4th & 5th.

Hall met and we had a glorious time in the afternoon, but in the evening, but few were present, and we had a "stag debate." Sent to Cincinnati by "Red" Morrison for some French books. John Morrison was expelled, for fixing the faculty bench so as to give Prof. Elliott a fall in chapel.[37]

March 6th.

Attended Bible class after Chapel. Sacrament was administered in the different Churches today. Weather fine. Health only moderately good. Retire to bed at 10.

March 7th & 8th.

Nothing new in college, except John Morrison has been taken back, who was expelled about a week since. It was discovered that he had but little to do with the offence which was given. Heard a sermon in the New School Presbyterian Church by the Rev. Fisher, D.D., from Cincinnati. He has decidedly the most beautiful style that I have ever heard.

March 11th & 12th.

Hall met; the principal entertainment of the afternoon was some communication through the anonymous box. No meeting in the evening on account of Church. Saturday morning chapel performance was rather dry, except the last by Dr. Anderson, i.e., his lecture was very witty. Attend church this evening, and wrote a letter home, one to Morrison, and went over my French lesson. Weather cold. Snow about 4 inches deep. Health not very good; I have the diarrhea. Go to bed at 10:30 o'clock. 13th. Sabbath. Attend Bible class. Heard Dr. Fisher preach one and a half hours in the forenoon. After dinner, I stayed in my room the greater part of the time. Retire at 10.

March 14th & 15th.

Attended all my recitations. Went to the drugstore and got a half pint of brandy; feel much better.

March 16th & 17th.

Weather has been warmer, but dark and gloomy. My diarrhea is almost entirely checked, and I feel very much better, attend all my recitations and had the good luck to get through very creditably.

March 18th & 19th.
Health very good. Weather quite pleasant. Spent half an hour in a very pleasant conversation with my old friend McMillan. Hownell is writing a "review of the senior class" for the anonymous box, which causes a good deal of excitement to find out the author. I believe that I am the only one with whom the secret is entrusted, and everybody says that I wrote it. Hutcheson came back today and was welcomed with loud cheers in Hall and Chapel. Chapel performance very poor this morning indeed. Attend a lecture by Prof. Moffatt on the British constitution.

March 20th. Sabbath.
After chapel and Bible class this morning, as I felt very unwell, I took a walk out to a sugar camp, but I felt no better when I got back, and have been lying down nearly all day. Pain in my breast and headache.

March 21st & 22nd.
Weather very disagreeable, sometimes snowing and then again raining. I missed two of my recitations only from sickness; feel some better now, though far from being well. Charles Brown, who rooms two doors from me, has the measles and is very bad. Attend a debate tonight in Chapel. Question, "Is every man morally bound to belong to a Temperance Society?" On the affirmative, Clark and Atherton; Negative, Brookes and Steele. There was more wit and sarcasm than argument.

March 23rd & 24th.
Another case of the measles two doors above me. Received a letter from R. Morrison, stating that he had it from good authority that I had been slandering him to some of his Tennessee enemies, and he said that if I could not clear myself he would not write to me any more. I told him if he could prove the charge, I was willing to become his enemy.

March 25th & 26th.

Hall met as usual and the third number of the Review was read by E. P. Shields, President of the "Anonymous Committee." After it, an anonymous communication was read under the name of the "Pigtail Review," but in reality it was aimed at me, as the supposed Editor of the other Review. No meeting in the evening. Saturday. It took me until nearly 12 to get through with my usual German recitation, so that I've done but very little in the line of study. Feel quite well. Retire to bed at 10 o'clock.

March 27th. Sabbath.

Stayed in my room all day, but could not read as I had company, and especially counselors in reference to the coming election in Hall.

March 28th & 29th.

Great excitement going on about the election of officers in Hall next Friday. Hutcheson is the Phi candidate, and he has such an unbounded influence, he will certainly be elected, unless the A's and B's lie most manfully. We nominate him so as to make him sign the diplomas of the members who tried to have him expelled last fall. I have had a very severe headache all day, but have missed no recitation. Go to bed at 9.

March 30th & 31st.

I have been quite sick both these two days; did not attend any recitation. Took a dose of medicine, and it has operated well, so I feel a little better this evening. I was petitioned by the A's and B's to run for President to sign their diplomas, as they have no hopes of electing one of their own men, but of course I declined on the plea that I did not wish to have anything to do with the intrigues of the Hall. In fact, I wish Hutcheson to be elected to bore them. Wrote to Pa to write for me to come home.

April 1st, 2nd, 3rd, 4th, & 5th.

As I have been unable to sit up from my last record until today, the 6th, my memorandum book has been of course neglected. I went to bed on the evening of the 31st at 8 o'clock with a very warm fever, and slept but very little during the whole night; the next morning I sent for John Hussey, a member of the junior class, who understands the Eclectic system of medicine, and he gave me a couple of doses of lobelia and afterwards kept me warm with teas, until the measles came out on me so thick that my face was very much swollen. He then gave me a purgative, and today for the first time I have sat up long enough to write a letter home. Wm. Morrison brought me something to eat three times per diem, and was very kind to see that I should want nothing. I have been at no inconvenience except too much company; it seemed as though everybody thought it his duty to visit me and sit a couple of hours every day. I now feel entirely well, except I'm very weak.

April 6th & 7th.
I have stayed very closely in my room as yet; do not go out at all except to Mrs. Hughes, my boarding house. Went to chapel this morning, but Dr. Anderson sent me back to my room, as the atmosphere is damp and cool. It is a great bore to stay in my room, because my eyes are as yet so weak that I can't read. Go to bed at 9 o'clock.

April 8th.
Dr. Anderson called up to see me this morning, and offered to let me go home, if I were to take my books along and study there. This offer I accepted, as Mr. Brookes will accompany me as far as Nashville. I have not tried to communicate with my father, as Mr. Brookes will start next week. Drew all my money from Prof. Bishop, amounting to $130, and have paid off my debts.

April 9th.
Hall met, and as Hutcheson (Phi) had been elected President on last Friday, his inaugural of course came off first. The A's and B's have been caucusing all week to contrive some way to depose him, and as they failed completely in this, before they would yield, the following members have resigned. Mr. Brookes had their resignations, viz., Isaac Anderson (O), Lawes H. Brookes (A), L. N. Bonham (A), J. E. Brown (expelled from the Deltas), J. H. Clark (B), T. F. Cortelyou (A), D. R. Colmery (A), A. J. Cory (tool of the B's), A. J. Chambers (A), Wm. H. R. Honnell (tool of bigotry), J. T. Haire (A), H. T. Helm (B), J. T.

Killen (A), George Lytle (B), J. H. Marshall (the Christian liar), P. McMorgan (A), A. J. McMillan (B), Alex McMechan (O), B. Mayo (B), P. Noble (B), J. C. Tidball (B), Alex Telford (B). Eight are seniors, and all voted against Hutcheson; 15 seniors voted for him, and these remained. The "bolters" have formed a Society of their own called the Eccritean.[38]

April 10th. Sabbath.
Attend the Universalist Church at 11 o'clock and hear Mr. Bruce, a student of our college who is the pastor of that church at Oxford. At 3 p.m. Mr. Worrell preached in chapel. Walked to the top of the college cupola this evening, and when I got to the top, I was so tired that I had to lie down. Determined to start home on Wednesday the 13th. Retire to bed at 8 o'clock.

April 11th & 12th.
Spend the time in making preparations to leave for home. Received a book as a present from Mr. Honnell and also gave him one in return. Mr. McNair gave me the "White Slave," Prof. Elliott a selection of poems in German. Went around tonight and bade the professors farewell. Retire to bed at 11 o'clock.

April 13, 14, 15, 16, 17 & 18.
I was waked this morning at 5 o'clock by Mr. McMillan, who told me that the stage was there waiting for me. Left in a great hurry and got to Cincinnati without any accident at 11 o'clock. After taking a view of the city we went on board the steamer Statesman and left at 5 o'clock. Arrived at Louisville at 8 o'clock the next morning, where we met Mr. Robert Morrison. Our trip to Nashville was very pleasant, and as soon as we expected, viz., Sunday the 17th, we spent at Nashville and heard Dr. Tapsley preach. I called on Miss J. E. Miller in the evening. Came out Monday morning the 18th.

Aug. 23rd.
After saying "farewell" at home, I took a seat in a buggy with Mr. J. B. Buchanan, and once more set out for College. Spend the day in surveying the City of Nashville.

Aug. 24th & 25th.

Took the stage for Louisville, at 2 o'clock a.m., and although it was raining exceedingly hard, we had quite a pleasant berth inside. We went the Bardstown route, and had very pleasant weather, so that we enjoyed ourselves very well, considering that so many were both inside and on top of the stage. Arrived at Louisville about sundown, and put up at the Exchange House. 26th. Was up very early and found my friend and classmate Ed. T. Shields, in company with whom I engaged passage on the steamer *Telegraph No. 3* to Cincinnati, where we arrived at 4 o'clock the next morning. 27th. Found no difficulty nor met with any accident on our way hence to Oxford, where I found but few of our old students but almost all new ones. My roommate has concluded not to return, and left orders for me to dispose of his property to his and my own advantage. Spent the afternoon in arranging my room, as I found it in a terribly dilapidated condition. As there will of necessity be much monotony in college life, I shall hereafter only attend to my manual once or twice per week.

Sept. 3rd.

As there have been about 100 new students to be examined, but little has been done in the way of either study or recitation. Wrote a letter home, informing them of my safe arrival. Gave $150 of my money over to Prof. Bishop for safekeeping, reserving $50 to bear my expenses this session. Wrote to A. W. Cannon in West Tennessee, and also to R. P. Adams of Georgia, to inform me as to the chances in each place for obtaining a profitable school.[39] As my former roommate, E. M. McCartey of Brookville, Indiana, is not coming back this year, I am rooming alone. On account of the cold which I took coming up the river, I have not been very well.

Sept. 10th.

My attention has been entirely occupied this week, as my studies have been somewhat onerous, and besides, the Miami Union Hall is at present at a rather low ebb, and consequently electioneering spirits are running high. Our Society has held no meeting as yet, as we are having a new Hall fitted up which will cost us at least $600. The Eccriteans and Erodelphians have joined hands against us, but our

prospects among the new students are cheering. Our chapel performance this morning was exceedingly good; all the participants were
members of the senior class. My name was read out as one of the performers for two weeks hence. I pled to get off, but did not succeed.

Sept. 17th.

Although I have been confined very close to my room this week, yet I
feel none the worse for it. Our new Hall is finished and splendidly furnished. We took in 12 new members, at this our first meeting. My
speech, to be delivered in chapel next Saturday, is written and has
been submitted. My subject is "True Greatness in Poverty."

Sept. 24th.

This week has been one of great anxiety to me, especially when I
would look forward to my speech; however, this passed off very well indeed, and the most sanguine hopes of my friends were fully realized. I
have also been troubled for fear that something unfortunate has happened at home, as I have rarely fallen to sleep but that I've had some
unpleasant dream connected with the family.

Oct. 1st.

No letter has been received from home as yet. Our election of officers
came off in Hall this week. My duty in said ranks is Corresponding
Secretary. Our exhibition came off yesterday evening, and the Hall
was crowded with visitors, who seemed quite disappointed, as the
speeches were very common. E. E. Hutcheson (Phi) and E. T. Shields
(Phi) were both good, but the latter was badly delivered and the former was an old one which some of us had heard before. Charles E.
Brown and Mr. Bruce were the other two performers, and neither of
them were very good. We took in only one new member this meeting,
Mr. Crane of the senior class, nicknamed Judge.

Oct. 8th.

No letter from home yet. I have gotten along as well as usual with my
lessons. Weather cool, but clear and healthy. Society met and elected
Thomas Williams, Jr., of Pittsburgh, Pa., as our speaker at Commencement, also William Dennison, diploma speaker. I have informed the
gentlemen of their election.

Oct. 18th.

The long looked for letter came this week, but contained nothing peculiarly distressing or interesting. Hall met and the following gentlemen were elected speakers for our exhibition in December, viz., E. E. Hutcheson (Phi), Thomas Williams (Phi), Theo. C. Hibbett (Phi), Crane, William Owens, and Henry Woodruff. Weather still cool. Answered Ira's letter. Also, in conjunction with Mr. Hutcheson, wrote to New York for *Le Courier des Etas Unis*.

Oct. 22nd.

Much excitement has been gotten up by the outsiders in our hall about the Phis "ruling." So Charles Brown has been nominated as their candidate for the next presidency, and as no opposing candidate came out, they of course thought that victory was perched on their banner. But when we met for the election, "Billy" Owens ran and was elected by one vote. How they tore! Today was given as a rest day, i.e., we had no chapel this morning. Winter has set in.

Oct. 29th.

The weather has been quite cool. Besides my regular recitations, and French, I have read *David Copperfield* by Charles Dickens. By a vote passed in Hall, we who are on the coming exhibition will be excused from attendance in Hall until next session. I have begun to saw and pack away my wood for this winter, but I find it very tiresome work, and am almost resolved to hire the sawing of it.

Nov. 5th.

Read the first volume of the *Life of Columbus* by Washington Irving, and study but little, as my duties were not very onerous. There was a show in town, but I did not attend it. There was also a woman's rights lecture by Mrs. Jenkins in the Masonic Hall, but instead of going there, I commenced writing my speech for exhibition. Thomas Williams, Jr., made a "nailing" speech in chapel this morning on "Chivalry."

Nov. 12th.

In addition to my regular duties for this week, I have written my speech to be delivered at our exhibition next month. Subject, "Means and Extremes." Wrote some letters, also. Minor Milliken of the senior class dismissed from College for impudence to the President, but was taken back after having made the necessary acknowledgments and confessions. Jonathan (Muddy) Stewart of the same class was also dismissed by Prof. Bishop for the same offense, but taken back in the same manner. Weather cold, health but moderate.

Nov. 19th.
Weather quite warm for the season. Read the second volume of *Columbus*. Gave my speech to Prof. Elliott to be criticized, with which he found but a few mistakes, and was much pleased with the sentiment. As I have not felt very well this week, I have turned my attention to taking exercise in the way of sawing wood.

Nov. 26th.
Weather cooler. Read the third and last volume of *Columbus*. Have not studied very diligently, but have managed to get along tolerably well with the professors. Thanksgiving Day was observed on the 24th, and we had such a good dinner that I have made myself almost **sick** with eating entirely too much.

Dec. 3rd.
Weather damp and cool, so that I have taken a desperately bad cold; put on my flannel shirt. Read the life of James the First of England by Lingard. Elected and inaugurated President of the Phi Delta Theta Society. Made a terrible effort in the way of a speech in Hall on the non-extension of the bounds of our territory and lost the question.

Dec. 10th.
My cold has become much worse, so much so that I'm kept awake almost the whole night by excessive and almost unremitting spells of coughing, so that by this time my lungs are very sore indeed. Have not been able to study much in consequence. Received a letter from my old friend James H. Brookes, who is studying Divinity at Princeton. He fears that consumption will soon decide his case. Read the biography of Charles the First of England.

Dec. 17th.

As I have not felt well this week, my studies have not been overly well attended to. Examinations commenced the 12th, and the senior class have sent in a petition to be examined first, which has been granted on the grounds that the speakers are from said class and ought to have some time to prepare. Read biography of James the First of England by Hume. Examinations of our class all went off better than usual.

Dec. 20th.

As I have been in a great bustle about the exhibition, little else has occupied my attention.

[Announcement pasted in diary:]
ANNUAL EXHIBITION
OF THE MIAMI UNION LITERARY SOCIETY
Miami University
Tuesday Evening, Dec. 20th, 1853

Order of Exercises

Music

PRAYER

Music

Oration .... H. M. Woodruff
  ″   What is Life? .... Chas. E. Brown
  ″   Render the Fallen Genius His Deserts .... S. Crane
  ″   Means and Extremes .... T. C. Hibbett
  ″   The Anglo Saxons .... Thos. Williams, Jr.
  ″   The Titans, with an Address to the Society E. E. Hutcheson

Music

BENEDICTION

The evening came at last; and decking myself in the best finery I had (which, after all, was my everyday suit, with a little of the lint, feathers, etc., abolished), and having received the best wishes of Mrs. Hughes and Ann Reagan, my boarding ladies, and the rest of my friends, we marched on the platform erected in one end of the Old School Presbyterian Church, accompanied by the best music the Acton Brass Band could give us: whilst thus mounting the stand at the sound of such delightful music, my feelings were so patriotic that I was almost beside myself, but when I came to take my seat and gaze over such a large audience (about 1,000), and especially when I came to think of what my friends had expressed a desire that I should do, my patriotic feelings were soon transformed into dismal forebodings that I was going to make a failure. Woodruff (Delta) came first, and made a complete failure: for he did not quite get through with his speech (which, by the way, was very soft), and, besides, he spoke so low that only a few near the stand could hear him. Brown came next, and had a very well-written speech, but had spoken it over so often to himself that he lost all interest in the delivery of it. Crane came next, and got up and made a first-rate beginning, but became frightened after speaking about three minutes, and had to refer to his manuscript, but as he was very much **excited,** and so **near-sighted** that he can scarcely read coarse print in daylight, he could not find the place on the manuscript and consequently had to sit down. In the meantime, I stopped thinking of my own speech to sympathize with Crane, and after listening to a very lively piece of music from the band, I got up and did the best I could possibly have done under any circumstances, for which I have since received universal applause. Williams did first rate, and so did Hutcheson, if his had not been 50 minutes long, when the audience were wearied out. Mrs. Hughes went to Cincinnati on Friday, and will be gone one or two weeks. I have been to the bakery and bought some crackers, light bread, tea and butter, and will do my own cooking until she comes back. The weather has been so cold for two or three weeks past that, although the sun shines out prettily every day, yet the little snow which is on the ground has shown no sign of melting. I leaped out of the room and strained my ankle so very badly that I can scarcely walk, which together with my bad cold (made worse by speaking) has given me the blues. Assisted Prof. Elliott in collecting the library books, and there is a prospect of my being appointed "Sub" in the Library department.[40] Received a letter from home which I answered "instanter." Phis had their supper in Clute's Ladies Saloon on Tuesday night, after our speeches. A full attendance was had, and Clute had prepared us a nice supper, equal to any wedding supper I was ever at. It will cost us about $30 or $40, and there were only about 10 or 12 of us. The speeches of the Eccritean and Erodelphian Societies went off tolerably well. All the boys except a few who have remained to study have either gone home or are visiting their college mates. I was solicited to go home with several of them, but refused, as I have more reading than I can possibly get through with.

Dec. 31st.

The vacation so far has passed quite pleasantly. I have been entirely by myself, except one afternoon in company with David Swing. I went to the creek to see the boys skate. I have scarcely been out of my room more than twice per day, and then only to stay five minutes. Have not been up town this week. Have read the first volume of the *History of Greece* by Grote, and one volume of *Don Quixote*, also the translation of Goethe's *Faust*, besides writing five or six long letters. Went to hear David Swing preach on last Sabbath. The weather has been warm enough to snow some more the latter part of this week. Feel only moderately well.

William C. Anderson, D.D., became president of Mi-
ami in 1849, and led the college through five years of
vigorous growth, to an unprecedented enrollment of
266 students in 1854, the year of his resignation, and
of T. C. Hibbett's graduation.

1854

Jan. 7th.

I have begun to feel that the vacation has been long enough, as the charm of being entirely alone has lost its enticing illusion, and the dread of the realities of my next and last session at College bears on my mind so much that I wish to see it passing. I feel now as though it will be a drag if I get through at all; I have not felt well this week by any means. Read second volume of Grote's *History of Greece*, besides some miscellaneous reading. Mrs. Hughes came back the 3rd and I was glad to quit batching. Received various letters from my friends who are visiting their paternal firesides, also one from Mr. J. H. Brookes at Princeton. Invited to a party at Dr. Goodrich's, but declined going. Weather cold.

Jan. 14th.

I make my record this evening, though I should be at a party at Prof. Elliott's, which it had been my intention to attend, but I felt somewhat unwell and the weather is too cold to be out much. Read third volume of my Grecian History, wrote a very long letter to my father, eight pages, also one of considerable length to Mr. Brookes. Wrote an article for the "Oxford Column" of the *Hamilton Intelligencer* on "the students' vacation."

Jan. 21st.

Our regular college duties commenced again on Tuesday last. Have made arrangements with the faculty about my studies, so that I will get through tolerably easily. James Patterson (Phi), from Hamilton, Ohio, has come to room with me — think I'll like him as a "chum."[41] Received a letter from Cousin Josephine A. Cannon, Columbus, Arkansas, which I answered. The weather continues very cold. Entered on my duty in the library this morning. Health is some better, as I have been taking some exercise.

Jan. 28th.

Nothing of interest has occurred this week, [but] my article in the *Intelligencer*, "The Sub-Freshman's Contribution," came out and caused a good deal of excitement to know the author.[42]

The Sub-Freshman's Contribution. — Hail the welcome notes of
the "Old College Bell"! Swing and Chambers in their places to
welcome their noble little band back! And a joyous time we've
had of it — been to Cincinnati to spend our Christmas (and our
dimes), together with clearing our heads (of all good sense), etc.
Oh, what a time we had there! Saw the picture of "Tom Thumb"
riding the elephant and the Siamese Twins on horseback! We also
went en masse in search of Uncle Tom's Cabin, as we had heard
that it was in that city, but we finally concluded that it was all a
"sell"! But this has had its place that we have not even time now
to talk it over, for when we "subs" get together, by the time we
get done discussing the merits of the different Professors and
hear each other's prospects, hopes, fears, etc., of ever getting to
the senior class (which is the Ultramethusalem or Jerusalem of
human hopes at college), by this time, I say it's generally study
hours; besides the talk now is, that our class will have to come off
in Chapel this session! It is rather an infringement on our rights;
but it can't be helped, for the Seniors are too lazy to perform, i.e.,
such is their plea; the Juniors can't; Sophomores are not required, and the Freshmen not allowed. So it is nothing but phil-
anthropic that we should assist. We are happy to state to the public in general, and the private in particular, that our college is
flourishing; a large number of new students are already here, and
if it were not for the classes above us, we would have no doubt
but that most of them would be in the Sub-Freshman class; but
we have no right to grumble, for if our class increases like it has
done for the last four years, we will graduate at least 75 between
this and the senior year. This is unquestionably and decidedly
without controversy the hardest term of the year on our class, for
I'll never forget the trouble we had this time last year (I mean
1853), i.e., that villainous scanning in Virgil. I mean the one written by Mr. Cooper, for certainly he was a scientific cooper to
have aggregated such agglutination of pure nonsense. So many
feet and other things which have not more to do with good Latin
than I have, and not half as much. It would have been a pretty
decent book if he had only left out the scanning; if some friend to
the students will get up an expurgated edition, without the afore-
said nuisance stuck on to it like horns on a sow, he will get my
vote for President next time. If the translation would only help us
out it would be easier; but it makes no more mention of it than if
it were not in the original; but I guess this is one of those beauties
in the original which cannot be expressed in English. And just
here, whilst I'm speaking of translations, I sincerely hope that
some good author will expurgate or rather expugnate the present

pugnacious edition of Livy, for the Freshmen say that when he
begins to describe battles, to give heroic speeches, etc., there is
no getting along with him at all; in short, Smart's translation of
Horace is the only Orthodox book in our whole course. As a general thing, the Faculty are down on bad translations, especially
when such are quoted in class, and consequently recommend
them not to be used to excess, being bad for the health and worse
for the grade both of morals and scholarship, except that of the
Greek Testament, which is recommended as a private manual.

But these things will come up more properly when we are a little more advanced in college and know more about what book-
keepers have in their desks; we are now more like half-grown
goslings on the very verge of goosehood, and the transition will
soon be made. Rich! as General Jackson said when he heard that
Clay was beaten in '44. Goodbye dear Editor; if our prosperity
continues, I will write you again.

Hall met and Charles E. Brown was elected President over Thomas
Williams. Seniors were excused from furthermore attending Hall unless they wish.

Feb. 4th.
The Erodelphians had their sessional speeches, at which I was present
by invitation of Mr. Manning, who read the Poem, which by the way
was a bore. Thruston and Hall had pretty good speeches. The Unions
and Eccriteans will be next Friday evening. A letter from my former
roommate, E. M. McCartey, in St. Paul's Minnesota, was answered today,[43] also one from Miss Martha Gooch. I am kept in the Library
every Saturday morning until noon, arranging the books, so that my
recreation time is but little.

Feb. 11th.
Sessional speeches in our Hall were held on last evening. All very
good, except Mr. Bingham in favor of Woman's Rights movement.
Theophilus McLean very good. A poem by Mr. Peck pretty good. C.
M. Hughes and Ransford Smith each did very well. We paid off $100
of the debt of $500 which the Society has incurred by refitting our
Hall. E. E. Hutcheson came back today from his trip East.

Feb. 18th.
Weather very unsettled. Health moderately good, only a bad cold. Re-

ceived a letter from Miss J. E. Miller of Nashville, Tennessee, dispensing with my services as a correspondent for the future. No definite cause or reason assigned. Her letter was answered very respectfully, and I assented to the arrangement with more joy than it would have been proper to have expressed. Thomas Smith, who rooms next to me, has the Varioloid [Smallpox]. President Anderson refuses to let the students go home. Another letter from Miss Miller, in which she seems anxious to have our matter settled amicably. She had heard that I spread the report in Tennessee that she had told me last May that she was engaged to be married. This in my answer I denied.

March 4th.
Prof. Stoddard delivered a lecture in the Old School Presbyterian Church on the late storm at Brandon, Ohio, which scene he had visited immediately after its occurrence. Finished the Review of Astronomy. Health improving somewhat, as I have taken some exercise this week.

March 11th.
Weather has been cool but clear and healthy. As I have not been oppressed with study, I have taken exercise and feel quite well. Varioloid has entirely left our college.

March 18th.
Tobacco Society started by the President, and Dr. Anderson and nearly all who used it have joined. I did not. George Dyche very sick in Charley Brown's room. I have not been in to see him, as I and Charley don't speak. Roomy visiting at home. Wrote to Cousin Josephine H. Cannon, at Columbus, Arkansas.

March 25th.
Have been very busy this week reading the *Wide Wide World*. A letter from home told of the death of one of our Negro boys, Houston. Also Pa's Steam Mills burned, an entire loss of all his lumber. Wrote him as cheering a letter as I could.

April 1st.
Another letter from Miss Miller in which she agrees to my proposi-

tion, that we shall leave off writing to each other. The faculty have giv-
en us a week's vacation, commencing with yesterday. I have squared
up all my back correspondence, having written six letters today. Spent
several hours looking for a gold pen, which I bought this morning and
lost before I had an opportunity of trying it. Health pretty good.

April 8th.
The vacation has not been spent by me as profitably as I had intended.
James Carson (Phi) is staying with McLean (Phi) this week, and much
of my time has been spent with him! Weather cool. The students, with
a **very** few exceptions, are back today!

April 15th.
McLean (Phi) as President, Bingham as Secretary, were candidates in
our Hall to sign our diplomas, against Thomas Morgan as President
and Joe Smith. The election was held yesterday, and I never saw such
an exciting time in the Union Hall before. The election was held in the
afternoon. McLean 19 votes, Morgan 17, one blank; Bingham was
beaten by Smith by a small majority; in the evening, however, we inval-
idated Smith's election, and Bingham beat him. C. Brown, President,
decided that the whole elections were invalid and I had to support
him. So McLean was run again and re-elected by a large majority. As
the opposition was to the Phi Society, we all became much excited and
personal and abusive. Williams (Phi) and Griffith came near blows.
The opposition fell "bored," and have been whipped on their own
dunghills.

April 22nd.
During the first two days of the week, we had a snow about four or five
inches deep. The latter part of the week has been very pleasant indeed. Wrote home, pledging myself to make no engagements to go
into business until further advised by my parents. We have quite a
busy time in the college now, as we are making an effort to get through
by the middle of May. My lessons for Monday are, in review, 60 pages
of Gizot's *History of Civilization,* 50 pages of St. John's *Geology,* and
(in advance) six pages of *Wilhelm Tell* by Schiller in German. Storm in
town, blew down the steeple of the Old School Presbyterian Church.

April 29th.

The weather very unsettled today, e.g., it is too cool to be without a fire, whilst yesterday was quite warm. Quite a busy time in college. The speakers from our class for next Commencement will be the 12 who grade highest, if they wish, and hence there is more studying done by some than is usual. As for myself, I care nothing at all about it whether I speak or not; in fact, I'd rather **not**! Health only moderately good.

May 6th.

Dr. Anderson cited me to a private interview, and after telling me that there was no doubt but that I would get a speech at Commencement, requested me to write the same in the French language, and also gave me the privilege of speaking English. Health only moderately good. Weather pleasant. No letters this week.

May 13th.

Our class has been engaged this week in preparing for examinations, "running reviews" in Dr. Anderson's department, and next week will close our connections with Miami University as far as recitations are concerned. In Hall, McLean, the president, and myself came at issue on some constitutional points which caused some excitement. Weather beautiful. Health pretty good.

May 20th.

This week closed my connection with Miami University as a student. After waiting for the arrival of Charley Anderson for two or three days, we had our examinations on Thursday, which was as good a one as we ever passed, and the committee were well satisfied. Dr. James W. Scott and the Reverend Mr. Maltby, (who took C. Anderson's place), were the Committee. The President gave the class a party on the same evening, at which all were present except myself; for this he gave me a lecture, and says his wife will score me again **when** we meet. Friday afternoon, I made an original declamation in Hall, which the President Dr. Anderson heard of and called on me the next morning in Chapel to speak it again. There were a good many ladies present and it went off well. My subject, "Bounds to a Nation's Prosperity." Dr.

Anderson saw me after chapel and told me that my speech at Commencement must be in English, as only a few would understand the French. Copies of my speech have been solicited by the students, which I declined giving, as it sounds better than it would read. The grades of the class were made out, and there were five between whom it was difficult to determine to whom the honors should be given. By reference to back grades, Mr. Williams, Mr. Hussy and myself were overruled, and Mr. Thomas Cortelyou took the first and James Killen the second honors. Jonathan Stewart was worst in the class: his grade 55. The 12 best in the class were appointed as speakers at Commencement, viz., T. Cortelyou, J. Killen, T. Hussy, Thos. Williams, Hen. Stoddard, D. Johnson, Woodruff, Ed Shields, D. McClung, J. Clark, Fred. Maltby, and T. C. Hibbett.[44]

May 27th.
Nearly all of our class are gone home or are visiting in the country, and for want of something better with which to employ myself, I have begun to write my Commencement speech. Subject, "The Political Past and the Philosophical Present." Thomas Morgan and Caspar Schenck had a regular fist fight about some girls. They were taken up by the town authorities and fined $2.50, and were suspended from the College. On the same evening, the students burned the squire and marshall in effigy, and to carry out the matter came back to college and burned both "Egypts."[45] The faculty now have the matter under consideration.

June 3rd.
Finished my commencement speech and have had it criticised by Dr. Anderson. No faults were found. Have a very bad cold and feel too unwell to do much, but write some letters and post up my books in the Library. Weather very changeable today, too cool to be without a fire!

June 10th.
Weather still quite cool. Cold beginning to break a little, but I do not feel well yet. I have spent the week in reading Ike Marvel's works, and have been very much interested in them. Among our American writers, he is second only to Washington Irving.[46] Wrote a few letters.

There was a riot up town last night between the students and town boys, who are denominated "reubens" by the students. I was in bed at the time, but the report is that the students were victorious; only three of them were hurt, and these not badly. About 12 of the "reubens" were severely injured. They broke into Jerry's barber shop and were driven thence and dispersed. The fuss commenced by some of the students being insulted on the streets. The boys will pay Jerry for the injury done his shop. The cause of the riot was that "Judge" Homes was passing along High Street, and as he passed the workshop of Irvin was hissed, and insulted otherwise. He stopped and inquired the cause, but they only cursed the more, when several students came up, just as someone called Holmes a "d—d liar," and Bob Berry immediately knocked the offender down with a club. With this, there commenced a general fight. Writs were tried to be gotten out, by some of the Reubens, but they would not swear to an affidavit.

June 17th.
My cold has gotten almost entirely well; and if my blood was in a good condition, nothing else would be wanting to complete my health. Dr. Barnett is giving me medicine, which he says will remove the malady. An attack has been threatened on the college buildings by the Reubens, with the assistance of the Irish, and as many country fellows as can be started up. So the students have kept watch and armed themselves, so as to be ready for at least 500 if they should come. On Thursday evening, Goodin, Barker, and Dobbins were stoned out of town, when a grand rally was made to go up and whip the town, but just as the students had all gotten ready to march up, the President came down, and after dismissing about 10, he succeeded in sending the others to their rooms. All who were dismissed went to see him the next morning and got back again. Have been reading *La Vie de M. Jean-Jacques Rousseau dans Français,* also "The Tale of a Tub" by Dean Swift, together with some of Byron's letters. Billy Owens, in firing a pistol, got a piece of the cap in his eye, which it is feared will take it out. He has gone to Cincinnati to be operated upon by an Ophthalmist. T. Williams and Gates Thruston have gone to wait upon him.

June 24th.
Feel entirely well, and have laid off my flannel shirt, and take a bath once per day. Billy Owens will without doubt lose his eye. Our Society, the Miami Union Literary, have been in difficulty with Dr. Scott about the occupancy of Tuesday evening of Commencement week. He engaged the church, but gave it up after we had taken the Beta's time on Wednesday morning. This caused a row with them, but it has all passed off well, as they have succeeded in getting Tuesday evening from Dr. Scott. A protest was passed in our hall, to be given in at the next meeting of the Board of Trustees, against the recognition of the Eccritean Society on an equal footing with us. I did my best to get up an excitement on the opposition, but gained only four dissenting voices. People have begun to come in for Commencement already, and we expect a large audience. Today has been a busy time with me, in arranging the Library and collecting the books. Did not get through, however. A letter from Ira.

June 25th.
Attended preaching in the Associate Reformed Church and heard a good sermon from David Swing; at 2:30 p.m., we met in Chapel, and after singing, prayer, and a few remarks from Dr. Anderson, we marched up to Dr. Claybaugh's church, where the president preached his Baccalaureate sermon to our class. Text: Genesis, 49th Chapter, Verses 22-24.[47] The weather was very warm and the house was crowded, but the discourse was good enough to receive attention.

June 26th. Monday.
Nothing going on except some exhibitions of the girls of the Seminary.

June 27th. Tuesday.
Commencement of the Senior Class in the Seminary. Dr. Thomas, President of Hanover College, addressed the girls at night. The weather was too warm and the house much too crowded to enjoy it.

June 28th. Wednesday morning.
We, the Union Literary Society, had our address delivered by Thomas Williams, Jr., of Pittsburgh, Pa., in the grove of the college campus. A

very large audience was present, and as the address was very good, strict attention was paid. As secretary of the Society, I requested a copy of the same for publication, but it was refused. After the address, Rev. David Swing made a few very appropriate remarks and delivered our Hall Diplomas. That evening, the Society of Alumni met, and all our class was elected. We had a great supper at Prof. Bishop's, and a good time it was.

June 29th. Thursday. Commencement Day.
Until 9 o'clock, the time for meeting, the weather was clear, and it bid fair to be a clear day. We met in chapel at 9 a.m., and after the Marshal had marched and counter-marched us sufficiently, we were all seated on the stage. After music and prayers, Mr. Killen began to speak, but only got about half way through when it began to rain. The rain passed off, and as it seemed to bid fair for a wet day, Dr. Anderson got up and announced his resignation as President of Miami University, and made a short but appropriate valedictory. Another cloud passed over and dispersed the audience, drenched with rain. We adjourned to the church, but did not get an audience until about 11 o'clock, at which time we proceeded and finished our speeches at about 3 p.m. Church crowded and the weather very hot. Thus ended a Commencement for which so much preparation had been made. The Baccalaureate speech came off on Wednesday afternoon, by Judge Hadley; it was a decided bore.

June 30th.
Though feeling quite unwell from the heat and excitement of yesterday, I was roused this morning at 3 o'clock to bid the boys farewell as they went off to Hamilton on wagons. It seemed like parting with brothers whom I was to meet no more. My roomy Patterson gave me a nice copy of both Shakespeare's and Byron's complete works. Ben Yocum gave me Hume and Macaulay's *History of England* in eight volumes. W. P. Reese gave me *A Dream Life* by Ike Marvel, and G. W. Berry presented me with a copy of *Reveries of a Bachelor* by the same author. The old college seems almost deserted today. Went up this evening to bid Dr. Anderson farewell, as he is to leave for Pennsylvania at 3 in the morning. We both cried at parting. The Doctor seemed

perfectly childish about separating with the students. I have the daguerrotypes of Patterson, McLean, Hen. Stoddard, Alex. Williams, Thos. Williams, Ed. Shields, and David Swing. About one dozen of mine have been taken. Mrs. Hughes has one.

July 1st.
Spent this day in packing up my trunk and loafing around town. Determine to leave for home on Tuesday next with Mr. J. M. Wilson, who will accompany me as far as Louisville.

July 2nd & 3rd.
Loafing around college, and cleaning up my room for Patterson, who will take it next session. Paid off my debts in town and drew on Prof. Bishop for the balance of my money. Went around this evening and bade the professors farewell.

July 4th. Tuesday.
Set out at 6:30 a.m. in the stage from Mrs. Hughes's door. I regretted leaving Oxford very much, as I never expect to see it again. Arrived at Hamilton five minutes too late for the cars, and had to wait an hour, at which time we left, but did not reach Cincinnati in time for the morning packet, so we waited and took the evening boat for Louisville. Quite a stir in town as it is the Fourth of July. Hunted, but found none of the college boys until 5 p.m., when we met C. M. Hughes and his brother, with whom we stayed an hour. We came down the river on the *David White,* and there was an opposition line with which they were racing; on this account, it was impossible to sleep. Landed at the wharf at Louisville at 6 a.m. After securing my baggage, we walked up to the Galt House and took breakfast, after which, going to take another look at my baggage, I found that by mistake it had been sent off on the Jeffersonville Omnibus to the depot of the Cincinnati Railroad. We immediately went in pursuit of it, but not getting across the river as soon as we might have done, did not get to the depot in time by about ten minutes to save my trunk a trip towards Cincinnati. My carpet bag was left in the depot, and they promised to telegraph and stop my trunk. After crossing the river several times, and being so often disappointed, it came back finally about 6 p.m., and the joy it afforded me

was more than a sufficient recompense for all my trouble. Spent a couple of hours with Robert Morrison, my former teacher at Poplar Grove Academy, who is now the editor of the *Herald*. Paid my passage on the stage for Nashville, and went to bed about 11 o'clock, but it was too warm to sleep with any comfort.

July 6th.
Was waked at 4 o'clock but did not get off until about 5; our stage was not crowded, and the day was comparatively pleasant, so that we enjoyed ourselves very well; towards night the passengers began to grow weary and sleep. I became acquainted with a Tennessean returned from California who was a real jolly fellow, and as the cholera was all along the road, we indulged in an occasional drink of brandy.

Mrs. Hughes' boarding house on Campus Avenue offered the best meals in town for Miami students, and also served as an omnibus stop for travelers to the nearest train station in Hamilton. The house is still being used today as a residence for Miami students.

NOTES

[1]Old-fashioned expression for "gloomy" or "melancholy."

[2]Robert Morrison was one of the six founders of Phi Delta Theta fraternity (second fraternity of the "Miami Triad"), and is honored by having his name placed first on the plaque which now adorns the front of Elliott Hall (called North Dorm at the time the fraternity was founded there, in Morrison's room, on the night after Christmas in 1848). Morrison attended the Associate Reformed Theological Seminary in Oxford for a few months after his graduation in 1849, and then went to Tennessee to teach in the Poplar Grove Academy, a preparatory school in Rutherford County, about twenty miles south of Nashville. He became Principal of the school in 1851, and as noted in the *History of Phi Delta Theta* by Walter B. Palmer (Franklin, Indiana: George Banta, 1906, p. 61): "One of his pupils was T. C. Hibbett, whom he induced to attend Miami and join Phi Delta Theta." Morrison attended Princeton Theological Seminary in 1853, but left to become editor of a Presbyterian magazine in Louisville, Kentucky. As the diary records, Morrison and Hibbett corresponded often during Hibbett's college days, and they met again, perhaps for the last time, at the steamboat dock in Louisville, when Hibbett was on his return journey home after his graduation from Miami in the summer of 1854. Morrison was later ordained as a Presbyterian minister in Louisville, and his church service took him to Missouri, as we know from Hibbett's letter to Prof. Robert H. Bishop, Jr., in 1887 (see Appendix B), which mentions that the two friends were continuing to correspond, even after the Civil War.

[3]This early form of "bus" was a large carriage drawn by several pairs of horses; it could carry a dozen passengers at a time.

[4]Clement Moffatt, Professor of Latin, is described by Walter Havighurst in *The Miami Years* as "a gentle classicist who wrote poems about his rambles in Scotland." When Hibbett arrived at Miami, he was examined by Professor Moffatt, who found that his preparation in Latin was not quite up to the level of his preparation in Greek and Mathematics, the other two major subjects of the Classical Humanities curriculum at Miami, and as a result of his examination by Professor Moffatt, he elected to spend his Christmas vacation at college rath-

er than to go home, so that he could be placed in the Sophomore class in all his subjects, and thus finish his degree in three years instead of the customary four. His extra study at Christmas was successful, as the diary records, and when Professor Moffatt examined him again in January, he became a full-fledged Sophomore. Obviously, his preparation for college at Poplar Grove Academy in Tennessee, under Robert Morrison's friendly guidance, had been exceptionally good.

[5]Charles Elliott, who was Professor of Greek at Miami, moved into the North Dorm with his wife in 1849, as one of the measures to restore order after the Snowball Rebellion of the previous winter. He and his wife were courteous hosts, often inviting students to tea in their rooms, as the diary attests. The dorm was later named Elliott Hall for him.

[6]Thomas Matthews (who died during Hibbett's second year at Miami, as we learn from the diary) was Professor of Mathematics at Miami, and had previously served as a civil engineer for the State of Ohio, surveying the line for the Ohio and Erie Canal.

[7]Dr. William C. Anderson came to Miami in 1849, as its fourth president, in the wake of the disastrous consequences of the Snowball Rebellion of 1848, when most of the senior class had been dismissed and the fraternities had been outlawed. In tribute to him, Ophia Smith says in *Old Oxford Houses and the People who Lived in Them,* that "Anderson had found Miami with only 25 students, the buildings dilapidated, and the grounds much out of order. In 1854, Miami had 266 students, the largest in her history." And in *The Miami Years,* Walter Havighurst gives President Anderson, "a tall, blond, handsome, courtly man," credit for restoring the morale of the institution and starting a period of growth that lasted until the year 1854, when Hibbett graduated and Pres. Anderson (tearfully, according to the account in the diary) left for a pastorate in Chillicothe, Ohio. It was in 1852, at the end of Hibbett's first year at Miami, that Dr. Anderson decided to give the fraternities official recognition once again showing his confidence in the students, who, as the diary makes clear, held him in high regard and affection.

[8]The Whigs were the rivals of the Democratic Party, and were successful in the presidential election of 1849, when Gen. Zachary Taylor of Mexican War fame was the Whig candidate. The Whigs had in 1840

sent William Henry Harrison to the White House, and later, when the Whigs became the Republican Party, sent Abraham Lincoln to the White House in 1860, and Benjamin Harrison in 1888.

[9]The Presbyterians had a major influence in the early history of Miami, since the first president, Robert H. Bishop, was a Presbyterian minister, and so were his successors through William C. Anderson; indeed, says Walter Havighurst in *The Miami Years*, "From the start, Miami had been a religious college, the principal training ground of Presbyterian ministers in Ohio." The Presbyterian Church in the USA had split in 1837 into two groups, calling themselves the Old School and the New School. The New School was a predominantly Northern church with antislavery sentiments, while the Old School had its strength among the Scottish and Scotch-Irish congregations of the South. The split between the Northern and Southern branches of the Presbyterian Church hardened after the Civil War, and it was not until 1982 that a United Presbyterian Church was finally formed. Rev. Daniel Tenney (correct spelling), pastor of the New School Presbyterian Church, became the principal founder of the Western Female Seminary (later Western College for Women) in 1853, while Hibbett was at Miami, though Western did not officially open until 1855, the year after his graduation. The Tenney Gates, built in Rev. Tenney's honor in 1954, now lead from Patterson Avenue to the Western College Campus and the new Miami Art Museum.

[10]The Miami Union Literary Society was one of the two original debating societies at Old Miami, the other being the Erodelphian; however, it was during Hibbett's college years that some disgruntled members of the Union seceded to form a third debating society, which they called the Eccritean. Each society met regularly for formal debates on issues of the day, and annually held an "Exhibition" in public, when the rival society and others gathered to hear speeches by the leading orators chosen by the society. Hibbett served as Recording Secretary of the Miami Union in his second year, and as Corresponding Secretary in his third and final year, and was chosen as one of the principal speakers for the Exhibition given by the Union on December 20, 1853. He wrote the minutes in the Record Book of the Miami Union Literary Society (now preserved in the Special Collections Room of the King Library) from Oct. 29, 1852, until March 25, 1853, and was

an active member throughout his three years of college, frequently
mentioned in the Record Book as a speaker and officer of the club.

[11]"Old Bobby" Bishop was the son of the first Miami president,
Robert H. Bishop, and a favorite professor of many Miami students,
including Hibbett, as the diary indicates, and as a letter written by
Hibbett to Prof. Bishop, long after his college days, further attests (see
Appendix B).

[12]Mrs. Hughes was the widow of Dr. J. R. Hughs (he spelled it
without the "e"), whose home became the leading boarding house in
Oxford, located just west of the campus on what is now Campus Avenue. According to Ophia Smith's account in *Old Oxford Houses,* "It
was not an ordinary boarding house. Faculty and students considered
it the best in town. Seniors engaged board a year or two in advance, for
it was considered the apogee of a college career at Old Miami to board
with Mrs. Hughes in the senior year." Mrs. Hughes presided at the table herself, and the food was served by "a tiny Irish woman" named
Ann Reagan, who was famous for her cooking. Among her boarders in
the 1850s, besides Hibbett, Mrs. Hughes counted Benjamin Harrison
and David Swing, and as the diary shows, she took an interest in the
activities of all who had the privilege of dining at her table while they
were students. The Hughes house still stands, in use as a student residence now.

[13]The Fugitive Slave Law was a highly controversial provision for
the capture and return of escaped slaves, one of the repressive measures that led to the Civil War. It may seem surprising that the college
students who debated this law at Miami in 1852 would vote against re-
pealing it, but it should be remembered that the student body was
about evenly divided between Southern and Northern students at that
time. As Rev. David Swing explained much later on, when he remi-
nisced about "Old Miami" in his column of July 14, 1877, in *The
Chicago Alliance,* a weekly religious magazine: "In all the years from
1825 to 1860, the Southern States sent their sons north to college, and
as the Miami University was on the border, and was of easy access by
the Ohio and Mississippi, it became popular among the high families
of Tennessee and Alabama and Mississippi and Kentucky. When the
South seceded, the sons of the rebel states went home to fight under
the Confederate flag."

[14]Thomas Babington Macaulay's *History of England* began appearing in 1849, and was acclaimed both in England and America as the most definitive, as well as the most literate, English history up to that time. This entry is the first indication of Hibbett's strong literary interests, which led him to read many of the classics of English and American literature on his own, while he was studying Greek and Latin classics in the classroom. In fact, his leisure reading during his three years of college was phenomenal, and it is no wonder that in his senior year Professor Elliott enlisted his help in keeping the library books in order.

[15]Louis (or Lajos) Kossuth (1802-94) was the most celebrated Hungarian patriot of his day, who in 1848-49 led a revolution against Austrian rule and became the leader of a free state, until the Russians intervened in support of Austria, and Kossuth was forced into exile. He went to Turkey first, and from there to England and the United States, where his fiery speeches in favor of Hungarian freedom roused large audiences to the cause, but the cause did not succeed, and Kossuth was forced to live as a hero in exile until his death.

[16]The name for the old-fashioned "privy," or outhouse, the only form of plumbing available to students in Hibbett's time.

[17]Benjamin Harrison is mentioned only once in the diary, although he and Hibbett must have been well acquainted, since Harrison was Corresponding Secretary of the Miami Union Literary Society when Hibbett joined it in the fall of 1851, and was a member of Phi Delta Theta fraternity, as well as a regular boarder at Mrs. Hughes' boarding house. Harrison was the grandson of a president, William Henry Harrison, whose term of office had lasted only a few months after his election in 1840; 36 years after Benjamin Harrison graduated from Miami in 1852, he would become the most famous alumnus of the university, upon his election as 23rd President of the United States in 1888.

[18]Jeremiah Morrow was one of the earliest promoters of Miami University, and it was he who, in the summer of 1803, along with William Ludlow, "splashed through creeks of Butler County and selected a wild township on Four Mile Creek" as a site for the prospective college; this township, within the Symmes Purchase, would later be named Oxford, and in 1809, to continue the account given by Walter Havighurst in *The Miami Years,* Morrow went back to the site as

one of the 20 members of the newly constituted Board of Trustees to make the choice official.

[19]Orange Nash Stoddard, Professor of Natural Sciences at Miami for 25 years, was popularly known as the "Little Magician" for his dramatic demonstrations of chemistry and magnetism in the classroom. The South Dormitory was later named Stoddard Hall in his honor.

[20]This entry is Hibbett's first reference to the college fraternities, which were such an important part of Old Miami student life that the college became known as the "Mother of Fraternities." But the fraternities had fallen out of favor with the authorities because of the part they played in the Snowball Rebellion of 1848, and they were forced to continue *sub rosa* until the summer of 1852, when President Anderson recognized them officially — only a couple of months after Hibbett mentions the "secret societies" in his diary. Since Hibbett had been brought to Miami by Robert Morrison, the founder of Phi Delta Theta, he was naturally friendly with the fraternity members, but to his credit, although he did attend one secret meeting to discuss strategy in the Union Literary Society debates, he declined an invitation to join them while they were still under censure. In fact, he was critical of the secret societies in his first year, and joined with other non-Greeks in setting up a mock-fraternity called Kappa Gamma Theta, a deliberate burlesque of the secret clubs. In the fall of 1852, however, at the beginning of his second year at Miami, he accepted the invitation to become a member of Phi Delta Theta, which was now officially sanctioned, and took such an active part that later that same year he was elected secretary of the chapter, and then, in his third and final year, he was elected president of the fraternity.

[21]Besides Phi Delta Theta, the two earliest Miami fraternities were the Alpha Delta Phis and the Beta Theta Pis. The "Alphas" had come to Miami in 1835 from Hamilton College in New York; the "Betas" had been founded by a group of Miami students in 1839. Both of these fraternities had been suspended because of their participation in the Snowball Rebellion of 1848. Phi Delta Theta, having been formed after the Snowball Rebellion, was the first to receive official recognition in 1852; later, recognition was granted to other fraternities — even including Delta Kappa Epsilon (the "Dekes"), which was colonized in

1852 from a group of Phi Delta Thetas expelled for drunkenness.

[22]Clute's Bakery and Saloon was a favorite dining place for Miami students during Hibbett's college years, and a place where on special occasions celebratory banquets were held. An advertisement in the *Hamilton Intelligencer* of that day reads: "Clute's Bakery and Saloons, Southeast Corner, Public Square, Oxford, Ohio. Oysters and ice cream in season, confectioneries, toys, variety goods, groceries, etc., always on hand very low for cash."

[23]John Lindley was one of the six founders of Phi Delta Theta.

[24]Dr. John Witherspoon Scott had been a professor of science in the early days of Miami, and returned to Oxford in 1849 to found the Oxford Female Institute. His daughter, Caroline Scott, married Benjamin Harrison in 1853 — one proof of the friendly relations between Oxford's male and female colleges, even before co-education became accepted later in the century. From the diary, it is apparent that the boys of Miami and the girls of Oxford College frequently attended each other's public meetings, such as chapel services, literary exhibitions, and commencement exercises.

[25]James K. Polk of Tennessee had been President of the United States from 1844-48; after his death in 1850, his tomb in Nashville became a place of pilgrimage, as Hibbett's diary shows.

[26]A hack was a horse-drawn carriage, the original of the "hackney-cab" or taxi; Hibbett used it to get from the hotel to the railroad station.

[27]Lavergne was a town about twenty miles southwest of Nashville, the nearest settlement to the Hibbett farm.

[28]Harriet Beecher Stowe's *Uncle Tom's Cabin* was a sensational best-seller in 1852, the year Hibbett mentions reading it at Miami; surprisingly, he makes no comment on his response, although later on, in 1854, when he wrote a column for the *Hamilton Intelligencer* about the Christmas vacation at Miami, he made humorous reference to the college boys' vain search in Cincinnati for the original Uncle Tom's Cabin, which was reputed to be located near the city.

[29]In April of 1852, the Phi Delta Thetas became too large to meet in a single room of the dormitory, as was their normal practice, and so they elected to split into two chapters, Alpha and Beta. David Swing became president of Ohio Alpha, and Benjamin Harrison became sec-

retary; E. E. Hutcheson was chosen president of Ohio Beta. The two chapters met separately, but collaborated in electing new members. Hibbett notes that he was elected to the Beta chapter but requested transfer to the Alpha; his name appeared as one of the thirteen signers of the Constitution of the new bicameral fraternity; however, in November of 1852, shortly after his initiation, the chapters rejoined into a single Ohio Alpha, partly because they were about to colonize a new chapter in Texas, and thus become a national fraternity.

[30]That a Miami student was initiated into Phi Delta Theta and then commissioned to form a new chapter at Austin College in Texas shows how rapidly the fraternity was moving from local to national status during the time Hibbett was in college.

[31]David Swing graduated from Miami in 1852, a classmate of Benjamin Harrison, and Salutatorian of his class, viewed by his fellow students as among those most likely to succeed. In *Men of Old Miami,* Walter Havighurst quotes this description of Swing by one of his classmates: "he was full of friendship, intellectual curiosity, love of beauty and moral earnestness. He was the most enthusiastic classicist I ever met. He knew his Virgil by heart and the *Iliad* was almost as familiar to him as the spelling book." Swing went to the Old School Presbyterian Seminary in Cincinnati for a year, and then, in the fall of 1853, he returned to Oxford to become principal of the preparatory department of Miami. His sermons in the chapel became very popular, and he remained on the Miami faculty until 1862, when he was called to Chicago to be pastor of Westminster Presbyterian Church. His preaching in Chicago was so popular and liberal that he was accused by a fellow Presbyterian of "heterodoxy" and forced to stand trial, but he survived the controversy and became nationally famous; at the Central Church in Chicago, his congregation numbered in the thousands, and his sermons were widely published in magazines and collected into books.

[32]The Maine Liquor Law was an early Prohibition Law, passed in 1851 to make the production and consumption of alcohol illegal in that state. Although Hibbett mentions in his diary that he occasionally drank brandy to settle his stomach, and held one egg nog party in his dormitory room to celebrate the New Year, he also attended meetings of the Temperance Society on campus, and was generally moderate in his drinking habits — in contrast to some of his fellow students, whom

he describes as getting "tight" and engaging, at times, in the sort of reckless behavior that must have made for lively debate on the Maine Liquor Law.

[33]Franklin Pierce became President of the United States in 1852. A former classmate of Hawthorne and Longfellow at Bowdoin College in Maine, Pierce had campaigned as a compromiser on the slavery question.

[34]The substitution of French and German for Greek, which was approved as an option by the Miami Board of Trustees in 1852, was the first step towards modernizing the old Classical Humanities curriculum, which had prevailed at Miami since its founding. Since four years of German and four years of French were to be taken instead of four years of Greek, this first move can hardly be regarded as a lowering of academic standards, though in time, of course, the study of ancient classical languages would be almost entirely replaced by the study of modern languages, including English. Hibbett was exceptional, in that he took German and French in addition to Greek and Latin, by his own choice.

[35]Hibbett's preference for Washington Irving and his distaste for Thomas Carlyle is interesting, clearly showing his choice of a light and humorous literary style over a heavy and oratorical style. Both Irving, as a living American writer, and Carlyle, as a living British writer, were much admired by readers of the time, but Hibbett's own style, as reflected in the diary, is much closer to Irving's than to Carlyle's.

[36]The practice of memorizing speeches for public delivery was common in the Miami literary and debating societies, but as Hibbett's hilarious account of the Union Exhibition of 1853 reveals, not all students were as successful as he was in "committing" their speeches to memory.

[37]The full account of this amusing episode is given in Walter Havighurst's *Men of Old Miami* and is worth quoting: "In the 1850s there were seven members of the Miami faculty, whom the students saw each morning at the chapel service. They occupied a pew resting on two endboards at the edge of the platform and a third board in the exact middle. A mechanically minded student saw that by pushing the pew two inches to the right where stout, benign Professor Elliott sat, he could illustrate the principle of the fulcrum and the lever. The ex-

periment was a complete success. As Henry A. MacCracken remembered it, 45 years later, 'Professors Bishop, Stoddard, and Wylie, all slight men, sat down first; then came Professors Swing and Hruby, their equals in weight. Last came the ponderous Dr. Elliott and as soon as the pew felt his weight, down went the projecting end to the floor and up in the air went the professors. It was a foolish practical joke — of which the author never became known.' " That the prankster was never caught is corroborated by Hibbett's diary — although there was a suspect at first, who was later acquitted.

[38]The formation of the third Miami literary and debating society, the Eccritean, was from dissenting members of the Union Literary Society, as Hibbett reports. He himself remained the loyal Recording Secretary of the Union.

[39]The letter from Hibbett's cousin, A. W. Cannon, of Tennessee, is printed in the Appendix.

[40]It was an honor to be chosen as sub-librarian to Professor Elliott, although the Miami library was at that time a small collection, and the library duties consisted mainly of reshelving books on a Saturday morning and cataloguing a few new acquisitions. Hibbett's studiousness was at any rate recognized in this additional task which was given to him in his senior year.

[41]James Ramsey Patterson of Hamilton, Ohio, was Hibbett's roommate in the final semester of his senior year, and later a wealthy and distinguished citizen who built a fine home which he called "Glenwilde," which later became Patterson Place, the home at one time of the Western College president and now headquarters of the Western College Alumnae Association. Patterson's name is also remembered by Patterson Avenue, one of the principal streets through the Miami campus, and it appears in the rotunda of the Alumni Library (now the home of the Architecture Department), which was built in 1909 with funds to which he contributed substantially. Patterson was a member of the Miami Board of Trustees from 1899 until his death in 1913, and in 1912 was granted an honorary L.L.D. by the University.

[42]In January, 1854, Hibbett wrote a column for the Oxford Department of the *Hamilton Intelligencer,* under the pseudonym of "Scribendi." This column was pasted in his diary, and is reproduced here in its entirety. Note that although Hibbett was a graduating senior, he

called the article "The Sub-Freshman's Composition," probably to conceal his identity and to affect a humorous naiveté for his column.

[43]The letter from E. W. McCartey, of Brookville, Indiana, Hibbett's former roommate, is printed in the Appendix. McCartey had left Miami to go to St. Paul, Minnesota, at that time a frontier settlement where opportunities for jobs were booming.

[44]The following announcement of the Miami Commencement of June, 1852, appeared in the *Hamilton Intelligencer* and is preserved in Hibbett's diary:

The Twenty-ninth Annual Circular of the University has just been published. The summary of its students for the year is:

Seniors	28
Juniors	23
Sophomores	34
Freshmen	48
Total	133
Preparatory Department	45
Normal School	63
Model School	25
Grand Total	266

The exercises of commencement week as far as made public will be:

The Baccalaureate sermon by the President, on Sabbath, June 25, at 3 p.m.

The Address before the Miami Union Literary Society on Tuesday evening, by Thomas Williams, Esq., of Pittsburgh, Pa., and the delivery of diplomas to that society by Rev. D. Swing.

The Address before the Society of Alumni on Wednesday, 3 p.m., by Samuel Galloway, Esq., of Columbus.

The address before the Erodelphian and Eccritean Societies by Rev. Dr. Orlon, of New York, on Wednesday evening, with the delivery of diplomas by T. W. Herron, Esq., of Cincinnati.

The commencement exercises on Thursday at 9 a.m., comprising addresses from Messrs. Killen, Hussey, Williams, Hibbett, Woodruff, Maltby, Stoddard, McClung, Johnston, Shields, and Clark, the delivery of diplomas, and the conferring of degrees.

[45]"Old Egypt" was the nickname for the long, low building which housed Miami's first scientific laboratory, where Prof. Stoddard performed his "magical" experiments.

[46]Ike Marvel, or "Ik" Marvel, was the pseudonym of Donald Grant Mitchell, a popular novelist and essayist who was regarded by many as a younger Washington Irving. His work has passed into obscurity, and now seems a pale imitation of Irving's style and manner rather than a successful variation of it.

[47]The text of Genesis 49: 22-24 reads as follows: 'Joseph is a fruitful bough, even a fruitful bough by a well; whose branches run over the wall: The archers have sorely grieved him, and shot at him and hated him: But his bow abode in strength, and the arms of his hands were made strong by the hands of the mighty God of Jacob; (from thence is the shepherd, the stone of Israel.)"

APPENDIX

A.

Two letters written to T. C. Hibbett while at Miami University

1. From his cousin, A. W. Cannon, in West Tennessee:

Dec. 5th, 1853

Cousin Theo,

I expect that you, before now, have given vent to many hard sayings against me for my neglect — that I ought to be burned for one. All of which I deserve and am willing to bear. You said something about teaching school and wanted to know the prospect for such calling in West Tennessee, which I can answer better by telling you what I have been doing in that line myself. I have been teaching for the last two years at the same place, for which I get $30 per month, which I think is as good as can be done here outside of towns. A new Methodist College has been established in our county seat (Trenton) and should the College be as successful as anticipated by the Trustees, there will be more Professors needed. I have consulted with some of the Trustees with reference to you. They promised me that you should have a showing. If you can get such a position, your salary would be more than above stated. You did not state to me whether or not you expected to follow school teaching as a permanent calling. If I did, I should not go to the country but to some town or city. I think that you can get a school in my neighborhood worth $30 per month, but can tell you more about it between this and the time of getting of your sheepskin. Write to me again and state more definitely your conclusion, especially with regard to your following the vocation permanently, or simply for the purpose of raising means to settle you in some other calling. I do not think it a pleasant business or suitable for you, neither would I follow it if in your situation. My

family have not been very well this fall, but are now on rising ground — except my little boy, who had severe risings
in his head and on his neck. He is a very pretty and smart
child. My wife lost her mother last summer, which I guess
you have learned.

The principal news item with us is the Louisville and
Memphis Railroad, which I think will be built and which I
think will pass in a few miles of me, if not through my land.
I am in two and a half miles of the Mobile and Ohio Railroad. The contractors are progressing finely with the work.
The timbers are to be laid by November next. We then will
have access to market, which is all we need. Lands are
rising rapidly — the same lands which could have been
bought when I came here for $5 per acre now command
$20.

Cotton crops are not generally very good with us this
season — average about eight hundred bales per acre.
Corn never better. I was at a sale on Saturday where it
brought but 80 cents a bushel at 12 months credit. I do not
feel settled here. I think that I shall go to Texas in the
course of a few years. I feel confident that it is bad policy
to be moving from place to place when one is well settled,
but I think that I will risk it once more. You must not delay
so long as I have done, but write.

Yours,

A. W. Cannon

This studio portrait, made probably around the time of the Civil War, shows Theophilus Cannon Hibbett with his first wife, Susan Tommie Johns Hibbett. It is the earliest likeness of him which has survived, for none of the daguerreotypes which he mentions at the end of the diary, exchanged with his classmates as they parted after commencement in 1854, has turned up — and no college yearbooks were printed until later in Miami history.

2. From his former room-mate, E. M. McCartey, of Brookville, Indiana:

St. Paul, Minnesota
Feb. 25th, 1854

My Dear Old Roomey,

Yours of the 6th Inst. came to hand today, and I hasten to answer it, lest we will not have time to exchange more than one in the present year.

This is such an out-of-the-way place and so distant from any civilized, Christianized portion of the globe, that when I send any message to the states, I am at a loss when to look for a return. I gave you Devil's particular H—ll not long since in a letter to somebody or other in Oxford for not writing, and began to despair of ever hearing from that hole of iniquity again, but you have some excuse in my unfixed and nondomiciled state, I confess.

Well, your letter was very satisfactory, I must acknowledge: why, d—n it, you didn't tell me anything, nor about anybody hardly. I should like to have had a complete history of the past and a probable conjecture of the future, for you must know that anything of the kind would be news up this way. You fellows of the Sunny South would like to know probably how we are situated up here, what we do for a living, etc., etc. Well, in the first place, we are bound up here about four months in the year by ice, and accordingly pretty costive, you think, etc.? Costive or not, we can't get out during that time except by wagons, sleighs, and dog trains — a diversified way of traveling: voyageurs and sleighs come up from Galena to Dubuque, however, every week or two, and we occasionally have arrivals from Lake Superior and Pembina by dog trains.

St. Paul is actually a fast town. It is as pleasant a place to live in (provided you have plenty of money) as I ever saw; there are about 4,000 souls here from all parts of the Union, and generally rather intelligent than otherwise, and considerable wealth in the place; we have four or five

Banks and a good many private Capitalists. This is the Capital of the Territory, and the Legislature has been in session nearly two months — it's rather a motley crew of legislators, some half-breeds among them: the **grande** question now under advisement is the Maine Liquor Law, but this is too dissipated a place in all respects to timidly submit to rigid moral dictation as yet.

I am told this is a very pleasant place in the summer, and is in fact the resort of many retired and diseased persons; besides, last summer it was honored with the presence of two or three English Barons and other distinguished nobility. They came up in part to have the pleasure of shooting buffalo a couple of hundred miles above this. If you want to take a jaunt after getting your sheepskin, you had better come up here on a short visit. It will well repay anybody for the trouble.

We have had some tolerable cold weather this winter. The thermometer was sunk several times down as low as 40 degrees below zero, and was in some places frozen. What do you think of that, Ole Tenarsee? Too cold for you, is it? In reality, I have suffered little more from cold than when at Oxford. The atmosphere is very pure and dry, and one can see a great deal farther than in the South.

Arrangements have been made to have a regular line of daily packets here next summer, and Congress has appropriated 1 million acres of land for the construction of a railroad from here to Lake Superior and the copper mines, which will be done most assuredly. Considering everything, I believe St. Paul will become a large place very shortly. The lumbering business is the main dependence at present, and the Territory does not contain a farming community sufficient to support itself as yet, and provisions have to be transported from below to keep us poor devils alive. Tell McClean to write to me, and tell him also, here is the place to catch trout fish and kill buffalo, and I shall be looking for him next summer with his gun and angling rod.

Tell Tom Williams he is a d—ned rake for not writing, and I am sorry he is a Pennsylvanian, for Erie riots will disgrace the Devil. Tell Hutch to fight the Eccriteans to the last and not let them floor him — please curse him for not writing. And finally, pronounce my blessing upon all friends and d—mn my enemies. You think Old Doctor gave me the high privilege of removing my carcass from his dominions, do you? Whether or not such a report is afloat, I care not, but that is not the case, and I refer all who wish to know to Dr. Anderson himself and he will tell you that he never took me to task about any crimes or misdemeanors, and that my absence was voluntary. Show this letter if you wish to my friends as evidence that I shall live to tell them I will drink their healths forevermore.

More anon. Write soon.

Yours truly,

E. M. McCartey

P.S. Excuse my imperfections, etc.

B.

Letter from T. C. Hibbett to Professor Robert H. Bishop in 1887, more than 30 years after Hibbett's graduation from Miami. This letter was found in the Special Collections Room of the King Library, among a large file of letters written in tribute to "Old Bobby" Bishop by his former students. The letter came after the Civil War had ended, and after Old Miami had been forced to close its doors for a period of years, but had reopened, with Prof. Bishop still taking his place on the faculty as the main link between the Old and New Miamis:

Lavergne, Tennessee
May 30th, 1887

Prof. R. H. Bishop:

My kindly remembered preceptor, until recently I did not even know that you were yet alive, but receiving a cata-

Professor Robert H. Bishop, Jr., known affectionately as "Old Bobby," was the son of the first president of Miami, and was a much-loved teacher of Classics through the final years of Old Miami and the early years of New Miami. It was to him that T. C. Hibbett wrote in 1887, expressing his pleasure in hearing that Miami had opened its doors again.

logue from my much loved Alma Mater, I find your name so familiar still on the lists of professors. Whilst a prisoner of war at Camp Butler, Illinois, I wrote to Mrs. Hughes et al, but got no response, but did not write to you. I am so glad to know that the University still lives and I sincerely hope she may more than regain her former status among the first colleges of the land. Would be glad to know what has become of the other professors and President Anderson or his son John. I sometimes hear from Robert Morrison in Missouri. Gates Thruston is here in Nashville.

I write this note to express my high appreciation of your abilities and success as a teacher, and the profit I have derived from the same, and also to congratulate you that the Good Lord has spared you and I hope blessed you, to arrive at a good old age. For my name, look at the catalogue of the 1854 graduating class. I have spoken of you to my wife and children often, and I hope your life may end as happily as you have been useful. I am,

Sincerely yours,
Theo. C. Hibbett

C.

Local obituary of T. C. Hibbett after his death in Smyrna, Tennessee, on Dec. 13, 1918:

CAPT. HIBBETT ANSWERS TAPS

Gallant Confederate Soldier and Sterling Gentlemen is
Called to
His Reward in 85th Year
Life-long Citizen of County

In the passing of Capt. Theophilus C. Hibbett at his home three miles north of Smyrna on December 13th, the county lost one of its oldest, most substantial and worthy citizens. Capt. Hibbett died after a week's illness at the ripe old age of 84 years and 10 months.

He was born and reared in Rutherford County, and barring the four years he served during the Civil War in the Confederate Army, he spent all his life here. He was a high type of the noble, Christian gentleman, evidencing the strictest integrity and honor in his associations and dealings with his fellowman.

He was a devout member of the Presbyterian church and a Mason. He was a successful and frugal farmer, following that occupation up to the time of his death. His 84 years rested lightly with him and he was in comparatively good health up to his last illness. He was twice married, his last wife and three children surviving, two sons, Messrs. W. C. and T. E. Hibbett, merchants of Smyrna, issues of the first marriage and a daughter, issue of his last marriage.

The remains of this knightly old Southern gentleman and war veteran were laid to rest in the Cannon graveyard, following funeral services conducted by Rev. J. P. Funk at the Smyrna Presbyterian Church.

The tombstone of T. C. Hibbett in Maple Grove Cemetery, Smyrna, Tennessee.

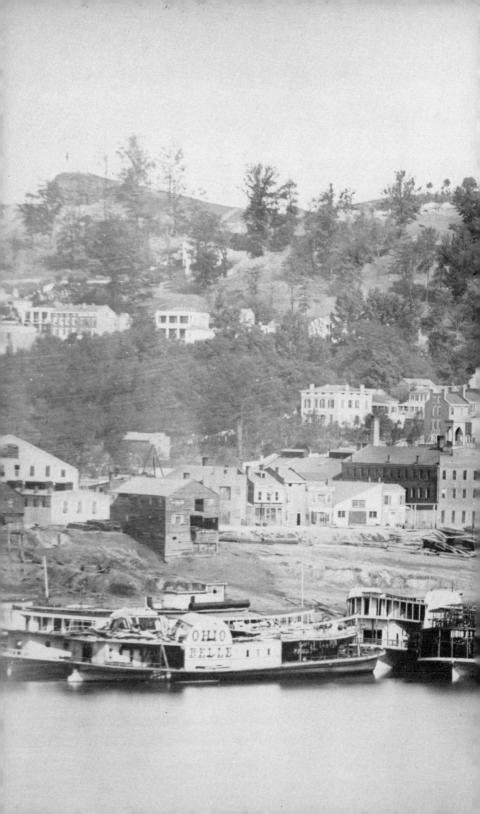